My Paddle to the Sea

MY PADDLE
TO THE SEA

Eleven Days on the River of the Carolinas

John Lane

The University of Georgia Press ⟳ Athens and London

Published by the University of Georgia Press

Athens, Georgia 30602

www.ugapress.org

© 2011 by John Lane

All rights reserved

Designed by Erin Kirk New

Set in Berkeley Oldstyle Medium

Manufactured by Thomson-Shore

The paper in this book meets the guidelines for
permanence and durability of the Committee on
Production Guidelines for Book Longevity of the
Council on Library Resources.

Printed in the United States of America

16   15   14   13   12   C   6   5   4   3   2

Library of Congress Cataloging-in-Publication Data

Lane, John, 1954–

   My paddle to the sea : eleven days on the river of the Carolinas / John Lane.

   208 p. : map ; 23 cm.

   "A Wormsloe Foundation nature book."

   ISBN 978-0-8203-3977-1 (cloth : alk. paper)

   1. Lane, John, 1954– —Travel—South Carolina—Santee River. 2. Boats
and boating—South Carolina—Santee River. 3. Authors, American—
Southern States—20th century. 4. Nature—Psychological aspects. 5. Santee
River Valley (S.C.)—Description and travel. 6. South Carolina—History.
I. Title.

   PS3562.A48442M9 2011

   814'.54—dc22   2011016376

British Library Cataloging-in-Publication Data available

For Louie Phillips

(February 12, 1959–January 14, 2010)

Friend and River Voyager

For whatever we lose (like a you or a me)

It's always ourselves we find in the sea.

—e. e. cummings

Contents

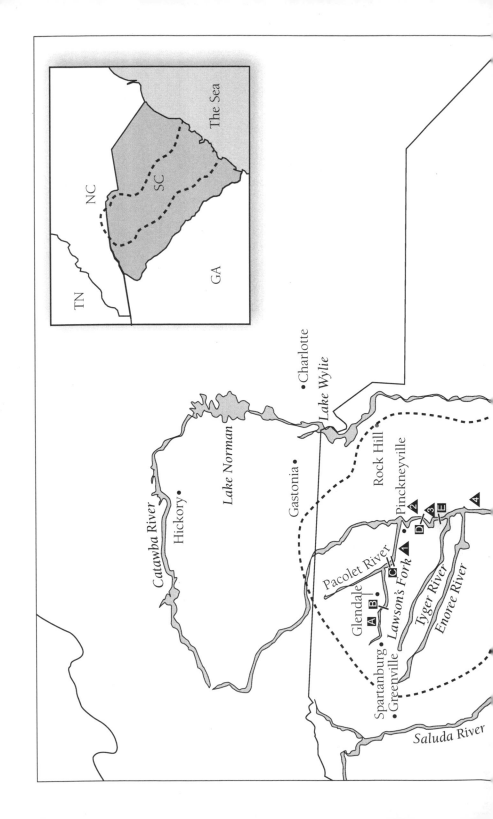

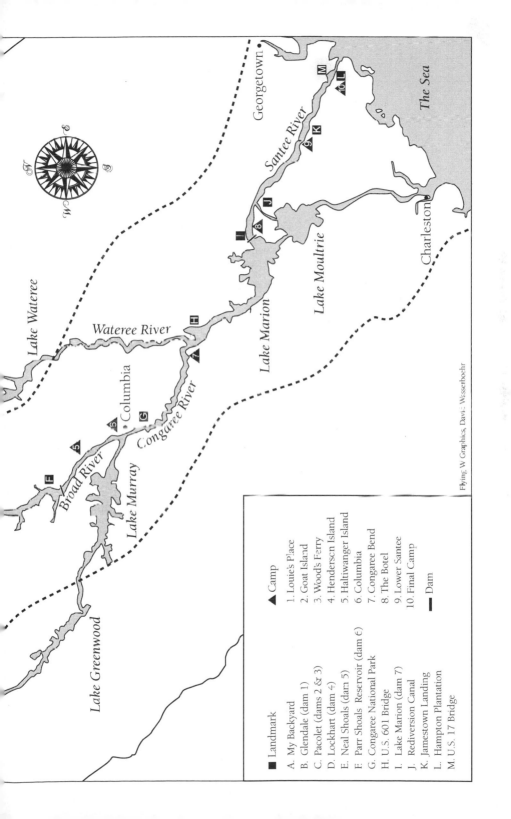

■ Landmark

A. My Backyard
B. Glendale (dam 1)
C. Pacolet (dams 2 & 3)
D. Lockhart (dam 4)
E. Neal Shoals (dam 5)
F. Parr Shoals Reservoir (dam 6)
G. Congaree National Park
H. U.S. 601 Bridge
I. Lake Marion (dam 7)
J. Rediversion Canal
K. Jamestown Landing
L. Hampton Plantation
M. U.S. 17 Bridge

▲ Camp

1. Louie's Place
2. Goat Island
3. Wood's Ferry
4. Henderson Island
5. Haltiwanger Island
6. Columbia
7. Congaree Bend
8. The Botel
9. Lower Santee
10. Final Camp

▬ Dam

Flying W Graphics, Davis Wesserboehr

My Paddle to the Sea

∽ The Blessing

From his spot at the top of the hill, Venable Vermont, with his long, salt-and-pepper beard, looked like John Brown or John Muir back from the dead. The late March air was crisp but not cold. "Fifty-five degrees with a forecast of rain," Venable called to me in the yard below, where I had gathered my paddling gear. The long-term weather report looked ominous as well. Weather.com showed cold fronts stacked up like green blobs one after another all the way west from South Carolina to California. Years had passed since I'd seen such a wet forecast. I watched as the big Alaskan picked up his dry bag and small lunch cooler and carried them toward the river. Then he came back for his boat.

Venable hefted his Dagger canoe up Northwoods-portage style, balancing it on his shoulders with his head inside, and took off down the trail. All I could see were his legs, his lower torso, his hands balanced on the upside-down gunnels, and the bottom swell of his huge beard bouncing with each step. I watched as my partner for the first eight days of my paddle to the sea descended our backyard trail. I fell in behind, carrying down the rest of my own gear.

I'd met Venable a few years before when he'd shown up with his mother, Martha, at a Spartanburg bookstore for a signing of my book *Chattooga*. He had been home from Alaska for several weeks to hunt, and we'd hit it off right away, sharing a love of rivers and literature. Venable's like no one I've ever known. Everything about him is larger than life—his beard, his voice, his adventures. He's local born in Spartanburg, but he's Harvard educated in geology, and he attended law school at the University of South Carolina. When he read John McPhee's *Coming into the Country* at age twenty-eight he took an extended road trip to Alaska with his brother John, and he hasn't lived in South Carolina since. He married a native-born Alaskan, raised two sons, and rose all the way in the legal establishment to assistant attorney general before retiring at fifty-five. Venable's no Alaskan back-to-the-lander, but he likes to do things back-to-the-landers do: hunt, tie flies, paddle canoes down remote rivers, fish for salmon, and smoke the salmon. Since we'd connected, we'd taken several day trips on South Carolina rivers and talked of an extended multiday trip.

Now Venable and I would be paddling together for eight days and about one hundred and fifty miles. On the eighth day, Venable would hand me off to my neighbor Steve Patton, who was scheduled to meet us at the U.S. 601 bridge on the Congaree River in midstate South Carolina. We'd switch out canoes there, drive around Lake Marion, and continue over a hundred miles down the old Santee River to the sea. On the eleventh day, Steve and I would meet up with two filmmaker friends in a power boat at the U.S. 17 bridge on the coast of South Carolina, where they'd shadow our canoe on the final push through the Santee Delta.

Long-range river voyaging was quite common in the eighteenth and even nineteenth centuries, when terms like *portage*—used to describe the act of transporting a boat around an obstacle, derived from the Anglo-French word for carrying or transporting—were in fluent use. The roads were bad back then, so people often took to the waterways. Everyone who has read *The Adventures of Huckleberry Finn* longs to kick back and float a river. "Low bridge—everybody down—low bridge—'cause we're coming to a town. . . . Fifteen miles on the Erie

Canal," I sang in elementary school. Does anyone sing that song in school anymore? First the railroads killed river travel; now interstates are the new asphalt rivers, moving freight from town to town. Old rivers flowing under bridge crossings are like ghosts.

The only thing that has not been killed about river travel is the restless desire that Huck felt to "light out for the territories." That desire to escape everyday life shows up in less watery narratives such as *Don Quixote*, *On the Road*, *Zen and the Art of Motorcycle Maintenance*, and *Blue Highways*.

By the time I lit out for my own version of the territories, I'd shaped my river dream into a personal river manifesto: Paddle if you can, but walk the shore if you have to; bushwhack, trespass, or tramp, but find the way the water flows and follow it as far as it goes. If you can do it in a boat, it's even better. If your stream is big enough to float your craft, you are in one of the last great commons known to mankind: navigable waters. As long as you stay with the flow, you have every right to be where you are, paddling to the sea.

Huck also taught us that paddling is very different from going overland. It's easy to fall here into timeworn clichés about water—that the river is life—or its source—and that the sea is a sort of merging with primordial waters. The sea is also a sort of death, if you take the point of view of the river. All linear flow ends there.

Several years earlier, paddling to the sea had become a dormant dream when historic heat and drought set in all over South Carolina. I had been determined to paddle to the sea by myself and had borrowed a solo sit-on-top Dagger sea kayak, bought lightweight gear, and stocked up on lightweight backpacking dinners. I'd sketched out a comfortable low-water schedule that would put me at the Lake Marion dam in ten days, where Steve Patton would meet me for the final push to the sea. But in early August 2007, when I was to depart, the temperatures had peaked at 105, with four days in a row at 104. That week was the hottest on record. There had not been a drop of rain in over a month, and South Carolina rivers were at historic low levels. As the temperature topped out that week, my wife, Betsy, had a recurring image of me sprawled along the riverside in eighteen inches of water trying to stay cool in the midday sun. I bailed out on that plan a few days before I was scheduled to launch. Not long after, I abandoned the entire idea of paddling to the sea. I didn't see how I could bring myself to do the trip alone.

Once Venable reached the muddy trail along the creek, he eased the big canoe to the ground. He stood in the misting rain, ready to depart, taking in the vision of the South Carolina spring beginning to emerge. The trail along the creek was a tunnel of newly leafed box elder, cottonwood, paw paw, and river birch, native species found along all the piedmont streams. The fresh leaves were all the more intense because of the misting rain. In a week or two the trail would be covered with fluffy cottonwood seed, and it would look like a late-season snow had fallen. I looked down at the thirty-foot-wide current flowing past and felt relieved we would have enough water to float over the sandbars and rocks of Lawson's Fork, the toughest section of our trip.

Eight or nine hours later we'd get to my friend Louie Philip's land. This first day was to be one of the longest of the eleven-day trip. We'd ferried most of our gear down to Louie's to lighten our load. What's more, the streams between my backyard and our first camping spot were small and constricted. We'd have to navigate through real whitewater shoals, a bevy of low-hanging trees, and three dams. In the rain and damp cold it would be a challenge to get that far down the river before dark.

When we reached the river, Venable said, "Make sure this throw rope is always accessible in our canoe." Venable gestured to the standard piece of river-safety gear, a yellow bag full of coiled rope. "We'll keep it close by in case we need it."

Venable lashed our gear into the boat. We had planned to leave at 9:15, and we were only a little late. I looked up and was surprised to see my chaplain friend Ron Robinson walking toward us on the trail. He was wearing his white robe and colorful vestment stole with his green rain jacket underneath. "I was afraid I would miss you," Ron said. "I'm here to bless your boat."

"Well, I'm glad you're here," I said, climbing back up the bank. "I can use all the help I can get."

Ron walked down next to our canoe. He wore L.L. Bean boots, a precaution against the rain and river mud. In his white, flowing robe he looked a little like a waterlogged Friar Tuck.

Venable and I squeezed in next to the canoe at creek side, and Ron stood at the boat's bow, looking out over the dark, watery scene. Ron's the chaplain at Wofford College, a mountain boy, part Cherokee. In his calling as preacher and college chaplain, Ron had blessed textbooks, notes, pets, schedules, and faculty manuscripts. We stood piously by as our craft joined Ron's blessing list.

In the misting rain Ron raised his right hand and said a traditional Cherokee prayer, with a little Methodism thrown in. Ron continued by reading some poetry he'd found:

A ruined river road forms our southern property line,
risks flood when the Lawson's Fork rises.
Yesterday walking down slope, I slipped off my shoes and waded
the orphan current, glimpsed upstream
a flowing, a future, and the run-off moving through.

I couldn't place the lines, but I listened closely. They became like a mantra I could keep tucked away for later in the trip when I might need them—"a flowing, a future."

"Where is that from?" I asked.

"A poem you wrote called 'The Half-Finished House,'" he said, surprised I hadn't recognized my own work.

I remembered the poem had been written years before while we were building our house there on Lawson's Fork. It had been my way of opening a conversation with my home place. Now, with this trip downstream, I was continuing that conversation by seeing what waited out beyond the force field exerted by hearth and home.

Ron was right in that it was a river poem, an anthem speaking of the uncertainty and risk of relationships with flowing water. The poem mentioned flood, and already, with the weather report, I was worried that we would get on the river and it would rise and force us to seek shelter on shore for several days, destroying my schedule. I was a college professor with an extended spring break. I had only an eleven-day window to complete the trip. Then I was due back on shore to teach my classes.

The chaplain stood and watched as we made the final preparations to head downstream. The rain fell a little harder, and he pulled up the hood on his jacket. Venable lashed our dry bags into our canoe. I stood by the creek and struck an explorer's pose, gazing downstream. "Eleven days from now we'll be at the ocean," I said. *Come hell or high water*, I should have added.

I zipped my blue life jacket over my blue rain gear. Venable put his camouflage jacket on top of his life jacket. He said the dry life vest would retain a little more heat. We slipped the boat down the bank and into Lawson's Fork and set out. I started out in the bow, with Venable in the stern. After I'd taken a stroke or two, I looked back at Venable. He'd pulled his hood up on his rain jacket. I couldn't look back too often or I might imagine a wild sermon as such someone from the nineteenth century might spew. I paddled forward on that rain-darkened, narrow stream.

ᗡ Rio Reventazón

This was the first major paddling trip for me since a vacation with Betsy
and our sons, Rob and Russell, had gone horribly wrong. Looking for a
change of pace for Christmas vacation we had set up a weeklong paddling adventure to Costa Rica with a fairly new outfitter we found on
the Internet.

The trip had started out simply enough. Jeremy Garcia, the outfitter
and a world-class kayaker himself, picked us up in San José. He was
maybe thirty years old, short, dark haired, and curiously dressed more
like a golfer than a whitewater guide—bright orange Izod shirt, navy-
and-purple madras shorts, white socks, and pearl-white running shoes.
Speaking little Spanish ourselves, we were relieved when we learned
that Jeremy's English was excellent. He was excited—almost bubbly—
about the idea of us kayaking with his fledgling company for five days.

After an hour's drive, he dropped us at our hotel, the Interamericano,
an orange cinderblock building on the edge of Turrialba, a town of
sixty thousand people in the Central Valley of Costa Rica, near the
country's most popular whitewater rivers. We settled into the first of
several days of a vacation routine of paddling, cold showers, beers on
the balcony with fellow travelers, eggs and *pico de gallo* in the morn-
ings, and hour-long shuttles to tropical put-ins narrated by Jeremy
from the front seat.

For the first four days it was all *pura vida*, Costa Rican for "the good life." Jeremy's father had been a raft guide in the early days of Costa Rican whitewater, and his uncle owned one of the oldest rafting companies in Turrialba, Tico Adventures. "Whitewater is in my blood," Jeremy said our first day, laughing.

Whitewater in his blood or not, Jeremy was a little of a hybrid. Though born in Turrialba, he'd married an American woman and lived half the year in Charlottesville, Virginia. His rafting business was only a year old; the fancy Web site, our hotel manager told us, was likely financed by his wife's American dollars and designed up north. I liked Jeremy, and I gave our family over to his preparations and decisions. This is what you do in the tourist industry. You trust your hosts.

We paddled progressively more difficult whitewater on our first three days in Costa Rica: the Pejibaye and two sections of the Pacuare. Rob, aged twenty-one, and Russell, nineteen, were strong kayakers, and I took turns in a kayak and in a raft with Betsy. The weather had been perfect, but on our fourth night in Turrialba, it rained constantly. When Jeremy arrived to pick us up at ten a.m. he said there had been a change of plans. Because of the volume of overnight rain, he had switched the trip from the Upper Upper Pacuare to the Florida Section of the Reventazón, a section he described as "class II/III." He promised us we'd return to the Upper Upper Pacuare on Saturday. He also said he hoped we didn't mind but that he'd taken on a few more guests who would be going with us: two geology graduate students from Utah, named Bryce and Orion, and a Costa Rican family—there was an older woman, a younger woman, a young man, a girl of about ten, and a tall gray-haired man who looked to be an American. We loaded up and headed for the river, but we weren't happy about the alteration. We thought we'd paid enough for private trips. This seemed an inappropriate change of plans, but we kept our mouths shut.

As we drove the highway over to the Reventazón I saw that it had rained hard the night before. There were fresh washouts along the road, and the creeks were running brown. I asked Jeremy if the river would be higher than normal. "No, normal flow," he said, deflecting my question.

What I saw when we arrived at the Reventazón put-in surprised me. I'd seen flooded rivers before. The current was dark brown, and debris drifted downstream—small trees, coconuts. The flood was not big, but it definitely was an overnight gully-washer flood. I commented on this to Bryce and Orion. They said they'd toured a Reventazón dam upstream the day before, and their host had mentioned there had been a large release.

Jeremy and his three Costa Rican guides loaded the rafts. I stood by the river with Rob and Russell, who were going to paddle in kayaks. I had decided to take on this river in a raft with Betsy. We marveled at the speed of the water.

"What's the flow?" I called to Jeremy.

"Eight thousand cubic feet per second," he answered, seeming unconcerned. "Maybe even ten thousand."

Even to an experienced kayaker, ten thousand cubic feet per second is huge. I figured that since this was mostly a class II/III section that everything would wash out to big waves and avoidable hydraulics. The last whitewater fatality in the country had been a decade earlier. What could go wrong?

The guides seemed nervous and took extra time with the safety talk riverside. They went over everything—swimming positions, paddle rescues, throw ropes (there was one in each raft), and kayak rescues. Jeremy explained how there were long, violent rapids on the Reventazón. A swim was not something we wanted to happen. The safety talk was good and thorough, but no one asked us to sign releases, and none of the guides checked to make sure our life jackets were secure.

Jeremy told us the trip should take about two hours and we would beach the boats and scout at least two class IV rapids. That surprised me a little. On the Pacuare they didn't scout any of the class IV rapids. We would run the first class IV, Upper and Lower Bamboo, before we ate lunch, he said.

About noon we set out on the Rio Reventazón. In my raft were Bryce and Orion up front, Betsy and I in the next compartment, and Jeremy guiding in the rear of the raft. A tall, curly headed Costa Rican manned the other raft, which held the other group of five. In addition to Rob and Russell, two of Jeremy's guides were in kayaks. They would serve as the safety boaters in case of trouble.

The geologists were experienced rafters. Soon as I felt the power of the water under us I was glad they were in our boat. We practiced our forward and reverse strokes. I felt confident we could move the raft around in the big water that was promised.

One safety kayak went ahead. This safety boater we called the Indian because he was dark skinned and had a very sharp nose and a nice smile. Behind us came Luís, a safety boater we'd paddled with on the Pejibaye on Tuesday. Our boys followed behind Luís. They were excited, and both had grins on their faces as we set out.

The first rapid was just below the put-in, a hard left turn with a big train of waves. We hugged the river left bend and missed most of the big waves, as did the kayakers behind us. I remember seeing Russell's eyes get big as he looked down into the terminal breaking wave, six or seven feet tall. Then the river took an even tighter left turn with a swirly eddy. Rob flipped but rolled up quickly. Hardly ten minutes into the trip, Jeremy pulled us all over on a cobble bar and said, "We're approaching Upper and Lower Bamboo, the first class IV rapid."

From where we stood I could see the constricted river sweep around the bend to the left. The rapid was so long that it was impossible to see it all from one spot. Jeremy and the guides headed down to scout the rapid, to look for the line down the flooding river.

"There's a big, big hole on river left and a very big rock in the middle of the rapid at the bottom," Jeremy said when he finally returned. We'd have to work right to get around the big hole, and then work quickly back to avoid washing onto the pillow rock. I saw concern on his face at what he'd seen around the bend, but he was ready to go anyway.

We sat back down in the rafts. By that time it was raining hard, and it made the river seem darker than it was. One of the safety boaters took off down the rapid first. Our raft followed closely behind but soon caught on a small rock. As we worked to free ourselves, the other raft passed us. Rob, Russell, and the other safety boater brought up the rear.

The rain pounded the surface of the dark river. When we came around the bend it looked as if we were headed down an escalator of brown-gray water spotted with waves and small pour overs. At the bottom of the rapid it seemed half the river was piling against that huge boulder. There was only one route through, a hard left ferry in front of the rock. I watched in stunned silence as the other raft, fifty yards in front of us, rode completely up on the pillowed rock, hung there for a second, and then dumped everyone into the churning river.

As hard as we were paddling, we were not going to make the move either. "Paddle forward! Paddle forward!" Jeremy screamed. Then, "Back paddle!" He probably saved us with that call. We landed in a hydraulic, and all collapsed inward into the raft.

Jeremy directed traffic throughout the chaos of our raft caught in the hydraulic. "Get the swimmers!" he yelled to the kayakers, including Rob and Russell, who had made it through the rapid. "Get the swimmers!"

All I saw was gear in the water. The lunch bucket and a yellow helmet floated past. Just to our right bobbed an empty life jacket, buckled up as if someone had slipped out of it. Betsy grabbed it and pulled it into our raft. The other raft was gone. As we floated around the bend and into the next rapid, we saw the little girl from the other raft clinging to a rock in the middle of the river. Orion reached out, plucked her off the rock with one arm, and deposited her in our raft. She screamed in Spanish and clutched her leg.

We worked over to a cobble bar on river right and beached the raft. Russell had gone downstream, along with two safety boaters, to get the runaway raft. Jeremy grabbed the throw rope in the yellow bag, jumped out, and headed up the beach, where he met Rob, who had pulled the older woman to shore. Jeremy took Rob's spray skirt, his paddle, and his river shoes. He stowed the throw rope behind the seat and made a quick count from the beach. He looked back at me and said with confidence, "I think we have them all."

I watched as Jeremy ferried across the river in Rob's kayak. I paced the waterfront. I was uncomfortable standing there without a throw rope. As a kayaker I'd never have gone on a river without one, but in that case I'd trusted Jeremy's raft company to supply what we needed for safety.

A cutbank cliff blocked my view of the big rock upstream where the spill had happened. Downstream the rapids continued for hundreds of yards. I stood on a big boulder, and I could see the second raft beached downstream on a cobble bar. I could make out three people standing with it. I waved my hands, and one of them—was it Russell?—waved back.

Our paddling group was strung out over a half-mile of river around two big sweeping bends. There were eleven we could count for certain. That left four unaccounted for. The initial chaos of the accident was clearing, and concern was beginning to build. *We could be here all night*, I thought. An hour passed. Finally my anxiety about the lost rafters got the best of me, so I walked upstream. As I approached where the cliff cut off access to the beach, Jeremy and his boat appeared in midriver with the two stranded rafters in the water, one clinging to the bow and one to the stern. "Kick! Kick your feet and hold on!" he yelled.

I ran down the beach following them but could do nothing else. I watched as Jeremy entered the heavier water of the next rapid. His red kayak flipped. He tried to roll once but popped out of his boat after one attempt. I watched helplessly as two yellow helmets and Jeremy's red one floated past and into the stronger rapids below. Two hundred yards below, just upstream from Russell's group, I watched as all three of the swimmers slammed into a high rock wall. They bobbed there an instant, then washed downstream. I lost track of them as they flushed into the next rapid.

We waited fifteen more minutes on the beach, stunned and unsure what exactly had happened. The curly headed raft guide suddenly arrived from downstream. He put us all into the raft—seven of us, counting him—and we descended to the next cobble beach, where the other raft sat. Russell and two guides were there, as well as the old man and the young woman, who had washed down with Jeremy on the kayak. There was no sign of Jeremy or the young man who had been in the other raft.

The old man pulled up his pants legs and showed me the cuts and bruises on his legs. "They told me this would be safe. They told me this would be fun," he said angrily. The young woman was crying. The old man explained, "Her boyfriend is the missing one."

"Where is Jeremy?" I asked.

"I saw him wash past the cobble bar far out in the river and around the next bend," Russell said. "He wasn't trying to swim, and he yelled something to me. I couldn't hear it over the roar of the river."

I figured that Jeremy had floated beyond the next bend and that we'd see him downstream on shore.

We loaded the rafts and launched into the torrent again, headed for a bridge that the guides said was ten minutes downstream. Russell was still in his kayak. We paddled hard. We were in shock. No Jeremy. When we beached the boats below the bridge, the police were already there. I figured Jeremy must have called them. But it soon became obvious that no one had seen Jeremy since Russell saw him disappear around the bend upstream. Soon it was obvious to us that the other young man, the boyfriend, had not made it either.

An hour later an ambulance arrived and took the Latino family away. That left my family, Bryce, and Orion at the take-out. We walked up to the bridge where there were three or four men looking upstream. In the distance we saw the curly headed guide paddling toward us. He'd caught a ride to the put-in to search for the missing boaters. He beached his boat and we could see he was crying. Orion walked over and spoke with him.

When Orion returned, he said, "Jeremy's drowned."

We huddled and hugged. Betsy wept. We walked over and told the curly headed guide how sorry we were.

There were so many unanswered questions when we left the scene. Was Jeremy injured in the swim? Had he blown out his shoulder trying to roll the kayak with the rafters clinging to it? How high was the river that day? Had Upper and Lower Bamboo changed drastically in the floods from weeks before? Was it the young man's life jacket we pulled into the boat?

There was nothing else we could do. The Costa Rica Adventures guides called us a taxi and we went back the hour-long drive over the mountains to Turrialba. It was almost six p.m. when we got in the taxi. When we arrived back in town we drove in past Costa Rica Adventures and there were already dozens of cars gathered out front. We tried our best to gather information through our hotel manager. I ran the scene over and over in my head that night in my dreams. Next morning we heard they had not yet found the lost rafter. Someone said he was an attorney from Zapote. We left Saturday on the first flight we could get out of San José.

Glendale and Little Five Falls

Now I was on a river again. About a half-mile downstream from our house a sheet of current slipped over the top of the Glendale dam. A flotsam of logs and beer cans was lodged at the brink. The rising water had made the flow turn muddy and thick. Behind the dam there was once a large pond, where picnicking locals from Spartanburg had paddled pleasure boats on Sunday afternoons, but it had silted up almost to the lip. Venable's father used to ride the trolley out from Spartanburg and fish in the pond when he was a student at Wofford College in the 1930s. Now there was nothing left of the pleasure pond but a slow, narrow stretch of open water upstream, creek-wide and hip-deep. Even the old pond's flood flats were filled with an impressive seventy-five-year-old floodplain forest.

We landed and stood on the shore of the creek in a misting rain and stared at the falling water. "The dam's got a nice gentle angle," I told Venable. "It's so friendly at the bottom. Local kayakers run it every time the water rises. This turns into a carnival play spot for twenty-something creek boaters."

The young boaters in the area call it "hucking" when you paddle over a waterfall and drop. The term probably started with skiing, but now it's used for jumping off any object in adventure sports—on skis, a bike, or in a boat. What would Huck Finn think of his name being associated with something so distant from floating placidly downstream on a raft?

We paddled downstream through the rain for several hours and came to a steep, mountainlike gorge where a series of shallow rocky ledges obstruct the creek above the confluence with the Pacolet River. I call that stretch of the creek "Little Five Falls," though it has very little in common with the wild quarter-mile stretch of class IV/V white water on the Chattooga River it's named for. I'd named the feature a decade earlier because it was long and had five distinct drops over river-wide ledges. The name stuck and even made it onto the descriptive paddle-trail signs at the creek's put-ins and take-outs.

In June 1999 nature writer David Taylor had put in at Glendale and floated to Columbia in a kayak of mine, which he nicknamed the Ned Beatty, after the actor who played Bobby Trippe, a paddler buggered and beaten in James Dickey's *Deliverance*. An essay David wrote about the journey, "The Ned Beatty and Me," describes a retreat from a bad marriage, a last goodbye to an eastern watershed he'd lived alongside, and a joking fear of suffering Trippe's fate while paddling South Carolina's rivers. David's journey was perhaps the first from upstate toward the coast with real literary pretense. In his essay, David reports lots of information from local river guides, but he also quotes literary luminaries Dickey, Henry David Thoreau, and southern historian of the piedmont South W. J. Cash.

David says that Americans need some sort of wildness but that southerners have rarely faced it. Southerners, he says, do not have to "confront New England winters." Puritans, for whom the woods were "a vast and howling wilderness," did not colonize the South. Cavaliers and Scots-Irish largely settled the region. For southerners, David says, "our wilderness is ourselves."

Rural piedmont and mountain southerners are often considered wild and dangerous. Take a look at *Dukes of Hazzard*, *Deliverance*, and even more recently, *Talladega Nights*. The villains that populate these cultural markers are often more scary than catamounts or wolves.

So why are those from the piedmont perceived to be wild? In part it can be attributed to settlement patterns. The southern piedmont, drained by the upper Santee system, was settled not by Cavaliers from the coast but by border people of England and Scotland who came down the Great Wagon Road from Philadelphia. These Scots-Irish settlers didn't like rules or regulations. They didn't want anyone or anything, including a church, telling them what to do or how to live. They arrived from Europe with little and cared almost nothing for recreating any of the cultural forms they'd left behind.

This theory is probably best articulated in the work of W. J. Cash. Cash came of age in the upper reaches of the Broad River and in 1941 published *The Mind of the South*. There he argued that the upper South, the piedmont we were paddling through, was victim to a particular kind of meanness and blindness primarily because of its settlement patterns.

The Mind of the South debunks the idea that the South is all moonlight and magnolias, plantations and refined gentlemen. Cash's South is mean and base and primarily governed and controlled by descendants of the lawless Scots-Irish. These were the people David Taylor feared a little as he paddled from Spartanburg to Columbia.

The Mind of the South has never been out of print. It still has a wide and diverse readership and is still assigned in colleges and universities, both in and outside the South. Some academics consider it an important primary source on the natural history of southern culture. Others consider it a scholarly embarrassment full of racist ideas and dangerous rhetoric.

David Taylor, like Cash, believes wildness resides in the southern mind: "If the dominant mood is one of sultry reverie, the land is capable of other and more somber moods. There are days when . . . the sad knowledge of the grave stirs in the subconscious and bends the spirit to melancholy . . . when the nerves wilt under terrific impact of sun and humidity." The insinuation here is that the weather makes us mean down South and that the land turns us wild.

When we arrived at the Little Five Falls the gray ledges and cobble beds stood out against the dark water and the emerging green of the stream-side trees. Between the ledges it was mostly so shallow that we had to drag our canoe over the sharp rock features. When we finally reached the bottom of the ledges, Venable looked around and said, "Walking our boats through the shallows is probably the most dangerous thing we'll do on this trip."

If you were a kayaker it would be impossible to live with a creek in your backyard and not think of paddling it in flood. High water means excitement and thrills. I'd hopped on my home creek only twice at flood stage, once a few years earlier with my son Rob, and the other time with both Rob and Russell. Each time we made the four-mile trip down to the Goldmine Road bridge, but not without incident, not without adrenaline at redline levels. The first time, Rob flipped in a big standing wave a half-mile above the confluence with the Pacolet River. He disappeared, and I followed through the wave and flipped as well. We both rolled our kayaks up safely in a big eddy, but the river below us was a minefield of boiling eddies and large submerged rock ledges with pour-over holes. After the flip, I put my boat on my shoulder and carried around the worst of it. I pulled out a safety rope. Rob ran on down, hugging the left bank.

The second time I paddled the flooded Lawson's Fork, the water was even higher. Rob and Russell and I got in trouble at dusk when we were swept under a strainer, an oak that had fallen and blocked the whole river. We emerged unhurt, but any of the three of us could have drowned. We were all well beyond adrenaline and into a shaky fear by the time we got off the river that night. I lost my boat and it was only after the river had dropped that Steve Patton and I found it eight feet up in a tree a mile down the Pacolet.

Then on this trip to the sea, when we arrived at the perilous place where my sons and I had found fear, I saw that the oak log had survived intervening floods. The log still spanned the narrow space between banks high over our heads. I asked Venable to beach the canoe just upstream on a sandbar. In the lower water the oak formed a natural bridge, not a deadly obstruction.

I hopped out of the canoe and walked a few yards along the bank, using my paddle as a staff to steady me on the rocky bottom. I was soon up under the log. Above me the old bark of the dead tree hung like a curtain in long, grisly strips flailed from the trunk by the passing floods. The bark looked like prayer flags or dirty vestments. I held up my paddle and could barely reach them.

Venable walked up the shore too and looked at the log, shading his eyes. "So this is where you passed under?" he asked.

"This is the spot," I said. "The pressure was so strong it launched me on the other side."

"Stand right there for a minute. I'll go back and get my camera. I should get your picture with it."

Venable walked back, leaving me there for a moment. I remembered a photo I had found on the Web of Jeremy Garcia's drowned corpse washed up on the shore of the Rio Reventazón. In the photo Jeremy's barefoot body was curled into a ball. He still wore his helmet and life jacket. A rescuer stood next to him and looked at the camera, a late witness to what had been a lonely tragedy. There could have been similar shots of us if things had gone differently. Wildness is not only in ourselves, as David Taylor had postulated on this very same river.

Wildness is also waiting outside us, and we stumble into it in a series of collisions. These mistakes and surprises are often what form a memorable journey, but they're also what make for tragedies. Venable snapped the photo. I kept my eyes steady and didn't look up.

Venable and I climbed back into our canoe, pushed off into the current, and passed under the log. Looking up I felt like a soldier returned to the spot of my unlikely deliverance, the foxhole where the grenade didn't go off, or where the rifle shot passed my left ear.

⟿ Pacolet Portages

Our boat carefully approached the first dam at the old mill village of
Pacolet. From upstream on the Pacolet River all I could see was the
dark horizon line from shore to shore, like a knife edge on the surface
of the calm piedmont river. The stream was dead in the backwater, but
I could hear the full force of the river crashing below my line of sight.
The dam itself straddles impressive granite shoals, which were known
in the days of the first settlers as "the trough"; the village Pacolet was
known until 1930 as Trough Shoals.

I knew from accounts of early surveyors that an impressive waterfall was drowned under the Pacolet millpond. The trough dropped
fifteen feet over a hundred yards. It was ten feet wide and fifteen feet
deep at the entrance and four to five deep as it expanded. In 1826
Robert Mills, South Carolina's most famous architect and an early
state commissioner of the Board of Public Works, reported that "the
velocity of the waters [at Trough Shoals] is so great that it is with diffi-
culty the shad ascend it. Notwithstanding their rapidity, several boats
have passed safely though the trough, and . . . taken their freight and
proceeded to Charleston."

Shad are schooling ocean fish that move up freshwater rivers to
spawn—what scientists call "anadromous"—and they run up eastern
rivers from Nova Scotia to northern Florida. On all present-day rivers

but one—the Delaware—their ascent in spring is blocked at some point by a dam before they reach their traditional spawning grounds. On South Carolina's Broad River they can't make it any farther than Parr Shoals Dam, nearly eighty miles downstream from Pacolet. What a sight it must have been to see wild shad leaping to make it up the trough.

Mills's is the only reference I've ever seen to shad runs so far upstream in Spartanburg County, and I found it both exciting and sad to think about. It allowed me to add another indigenous species to my imaginative landscape, along with the long-vanished piedmont bison, cougar, red wolf, and elk.

The power of the Pacolet River has been appropriated for human enterprise for over 150 years. Mills's map indicates a small gristmill stood at Trough Shoals, and later maps show a larger operation called Hancock's Mill (grist, flour, sawmill, cotton gin) operating on the spot. Hancock's Mill was located just below the dam on the north side, where we would carry around. It washed away during the 1903 flood, and in 1982 a local historian reported that its foundation and the wall that guided water from the trough to the mill were still visible under the dam.

I knew from prior experience that the best place to take out for bypassing the dam was on the high muddy left bank only a dozen yards above it. A dam is always an interesting river feature to approach in a canoe or kayak because it's hard to see what's going to happen from water level. The approaching paddler sees only a river horizon and maybe some rising mist from the water crashing below. As the water rises and slips over the brink, the twelve-foot Pacolet dam turns the shoals below into a drowning machine—if we were to survive the plunge to the rocks below, we would probably not survive the nasty hydraulic formed at the dam's ninety-degree base.

As we nudged the bank, I grabbed hold of several thin saplings. The canoe floated in broadside. My hands slipped on the slick saplings, and soon they were coated with red piedmont clay. More small, scrubby saplings crowded the bank, but I scrambled up and out, securing the canoe and stabilizing it while Venable climbed up too. Here and there other saplings had been bent double or broken back. Looking closer I could see that the bank had been stubbled with the abandoned, forked rod-holders of local fishermen.

After the gristmill of 1825 and later Hancock's Mill stood at Trough Shoals, textile mills were established and used the river's power. The first textile mill was chartered in 1882 and began operation as Pacolet Manufacturing Company the next year. In 1888 an adjoining four-story mill was built, and in 1894 a second dam and a third mill were built downstream. Today, the quiet village of Pacolet stretches up both sides of the valley. But on the morning of Saturday, June 6, 1903, it wasn't so quiet along the Pacolet. Three days of hard rain and a cloud-burst in the headwaters had sent the river rising to monstrous levels never before witnessed. The mill communities along the river—Fingerville, Clifton, and Trough Shoals—had twenty years of spring floods to recount by then, but nothing they remembered from years past came close to what rolled downstream that day.

Five miles upstream from where we stood, the mills at Clifton were wiped out as the water roared past and rose as much as forty feet in only a matter of hours. At the first Clifton mill, the water undercut the smokestack and it fell in the river. At the second Clifton mill, a third of the mill was washed away, the lower floors drowned. Just below that mill, the community of Santuck was inundated—sixteen mill houses in a floodplain bend of the river.

Men and women watched as their husbands, wives, or children were swept away. Some were washed as far as Pacolet, nine miles downstream. Cotton bales, tree trunks, cordwood, and shattered wooden walls turned into makeshift rafts. People on the riverbanks threw ropes or held out limbs to those clutching debris in the river, struggling in the current to survive. All day the rescues continued. Eyewitnesses reported that, in what was left of the ruined mills, muddy streamers of cloth flapped in the breeze blowing through the wreckage.

As the flood rolled downstream, it swept the Pacolet bridges into the torrent, breached the dams, and washed away or set afloat whole buildings, which were smashed to bits downstream. Wrecked looms tumbled from the missing sides of the mills and disappeared into the muddy deluge.

At about nine a.m. that morning in 1903, the big three-story Pacolet mill collapsed into the surging flood. The four-story mill adjoining it soon followed. Crowds of operatives (as they called the workers back then) watched from the high cliffs. Downstream another of the Pacolet mills survived, badly damaged. A church at Pacolet was swept into the current, somehow held together, and disappeared downstream, riding the flood, its bell ringing.

Along the valley of the Pacolet, sixty-five people died that day and six hundred were left homeless. Many bodies were never found. As one historian has written, "There was little to be salvaged. Most of the value was on its way to Columbia and the sea on the waters of the Broad River." No deluge since has approached the fury of that Saturday. "The Great Washout" it is called by the families who still remember the tragedy over a hundred years later.

My memories of the tragic flood on the Reventazón in Costa Rica a few months before and the stories of the historic flood on the Pacolet mingled like a confluence of currents that morning as I stood by the river. The sky was low, and a misting rain picked up in intensity. I worried that the rain would bring the river up and we would be caught somewhere below without enough knowledge to float safely through. I knew if I was to complete my paddle to the sea I would have to put such dark notions aside. For eleven days it would be the wild river and us.

Below the first dam, the town Pacolet still stood, a remote Spartanburg County village of about 2,500 souls. After more than a century of paternal mill ownership and governance, Pacolet now had an energetic mayor, Elaine Harris. I'd worked alongside Mayor Harris on many recreational projects in the river corridor. She had a farsighted tourist vision, which included reclaiming the riverfront and encouraging paddlers like us. She wanted cultural heritage tours, ecotourism with kayaking and canoeing. She wanted to create new industry in Pacolet, connecting to towns upstream, such as Glendale and Clifton. She'd said she thought preserving stories—like the ones of the flood—was how to maintain Pacolet's way of life.

From where I stood I could see that locals had painted the north end of the dam structure with a large Confederate flag and that someone had rigged razor wire to prevent boats from moving around the end of the dam. The area had a long way to go before Harris's ecotourists would float down the Pacolet River corridor with ease, I thought. As we worked slowly around the razor wire I told Venable about Harris's idea of preserving stories.

"Stories are great," Venable said. "But this isn't a friendly scene."

Rather than haul the canoe down the last one hundred yards, Venable decided to paddle it alone through a large standing wave just below the dam, squeezing out a little excitement for a veteran Alaska river runner. After I walked downstream, Venable sat in the stern of the green Dagger canoe and paddled past rebar through the gray river, directly into the upstream smile of the little hole and wave.

I got back in the boat in a big eddy. Looking back upstream, I could see that a day of rain had definitely begun to elevate the river level. A pounding curtain of river water came over the dam, circulated at the bottom, and flushed downstream. The water was rising, though it wasn't yet the muddy torrent I'd come to expect from a piedmont flood.

"How far is it to Louie's land?" Venable asked when we were back on the river.

"Three or four miles," I estimated.

I knew Venable had cooking on his mind. We'd dropped his Dutch ovens off at Louie's with the rest of the gear, and the plan was to camp and cook at the river.

"We've got to get those Dutch ovens down to the river before dark," Venable said.

Portaging the second Pacolet dam was more of a challenge than the first. The textile mill downstream is long gone, but the company still owns the land and generates power at the old dam. They've constructed a wooden apron on top, a way of increasing the amount of pond available for the generators by five feet or so. This dam is positioned in an even more constricted gorge and offers no chance of portaging on either side. One side is a sheer rock face, and the other is the canal to feed the little power station. There were signs warning us away from the canal, but I had developed a plan for getting around the dam on a previous trip to Columbia several years before that put us nowhere near their canal.

"Trust me," I told Venable and paddled straight toward the dam. "Aim for that thin sycamore."

Ahead of us the tree with its white-bottomed, ghostly leaves seemed to rise from the river itself. In reality the sapling was growing on top of a large rock outcropping that was incorporated into the dam.

We pulled sideways to the wooden apron and Venable could finally see the rock outcrop below the dam. There were still two inches of freeboard to the top of the apron, and once there, we held on and hopped over the waterlogged two-by-six frame onto the outcrop just below. When we had firm footing below, we pulled our boat over the top.

I'd worried all day that the river at Pacolet's second dam would be too high to portage and that water would top the wooden structure. I feared that people with authority would appear and tell us to get away from their dam, or worse yet, that we would slip inadvertently over the dam in a dramatic gesture as the river rose to flood level. But, as Venable liked to remind me, we were not idiots. We had not had enough rain to be swept over. "It's often better in river scenarios like this one to ask forgiveness than permission," Venable said. "If someone associated with the power company quizzes us about what we are doing, just say we didn't know."

In January 1969 Wofford College's athletic trainer Dwaine "Doc" Stober took seventeen students down the river from below the second Pacolet dam to Charleston. Stober's crew left a good journal in the Wofford archives with extensive notes on the journey, and I had read it before our trip. January is not the ideal month for long-distance paddling, and several times canoes full of gear and inexperienced river voyagers spilled in the cold river. They even had an evening visit from Henry Savage, author of *River of the Carolinas: The Santee*, as they camped along the shores of the Wateree, the author's home river. Their route took them through Lake Moultrie and into Charleston Harbor rather than down the old Santee River channel I'd chosen. Their account would provide little instruction for me once I was below Lake Marion.

I'd read Henry Savage's *River of the Carolinas* as I prepared for my own paddle to the sea. Savage's book, released in 1956, is part of the famous Rivers of America series that published sixty-five volumes between 1937 and 1974. The popular series was conceived as a way to tell America about its history through river drainages. Often written by poets and novelists, Rivers of America has proved enduring and instructive. Famous volumes include *Everglades, River of Grass* by Marjorie Stoneman Douglas and *The French Broad* by Wilma Dykeman. Andrew Wyeth's first book illustrations appear in *The Brandywine*.

Though I had previously read several of the Rivers of America volumes, I was not familiar with Savage's book until I found it at a recent book fair in Columbia. I was immediately drawn to it because the Savage volume is about my watershed, the river system that includes Lawson's Fork Creek and the Pacolet River. I hoped that by reading *River of the Carolinas* I would find a literary map for my own trip that I could update from 1956 to the twenty-first century. I hoped Savage would have laid out natural history narratives of the Broad and Saluda, the Catawba and Wateree, the Congaree, and finally the Santee.

Savage, a Conway, South Carolina, lawyer and early environmentalist, sketched out bold, vivid scenes of South Carolina history—coastal pirates, plantation farmers, frontier trappers, canal builders, war heroes like Francis Marion (the Swamp Fox), politicians like John C. Calhoun, and industrial giants like the Duke family, which had managed to tame the river for electric power, but the type of river lore I loved proved minimal in his text. There was no first-person account of a single mile of the Santee River system. Less than ten years before Rachel Carson's *Silent Spring*, there was little talk of pollution or recovery of natural systems. There was no first-person prose rhapsody about a single specific spot on the river.

Maybe I was looking for the wrong river when I opened up *River of the Carolinas*. I could not expect the South Carolina lawyer in 1956 to write like Edward Abbey in the late sixties. The restraints and expectations of the series and the period voice he found comfortable would keep him from the first-person point of view I preferred and practiced. But there was much to learn from Savage's mythic narrative. Savage's book focused on the human history that a watershed can hold, and it could prove instructive for my twenty-first-century nature writer's voice. "The river remembers!" Savage writes in his last paragraph. "But life, like the river, flows on and man, obsessed with immortality, looks forward into an uncertain future."

Below that second Pacolet dam was also where my neighbor Steve Patton had put in his own paddle to the sea years earlier. Inspired by Stober's trip, Steve, the son of Gibbes Patton, a Wofford College botany professor, paddled solo in a canvas and fiberglass canoe from Pacolet to the coast in April and early May 1981 when he was twenty years old. In his journal he'd written a brief first entry: "Put in this morning with the help of my father below Pacolet Mills. . . . Pacolet River has averaged 24 inches deep. Seen ducks, herons, cow. Lots of poison ivy. No impassible log jams." I thought about Steve as I portaged the second dam. Setting out on such a great adventure alone must have been a deeply exciting but also unsettling feeling.

For Steve, paddling solo had been an ordeal, and his soul-searching is hinted at in the five single-spaced pages of diary that he lent to me before my trip. At the end of his journey he admitted that he had been lonely and he reflected on what he hoped he learned: "I've learned to appreciate friendship in a new way. I hope to become a little more stable so friends I've made (and will make) along the way can depend on me for help if they need it."

I recalled a line from a Jim Harrison poem, "Looking Forward to Age": "One day standing in a river with my fly rod / I'll have the courage to admit my life."

For me it's not a fly rod that takes me to rivers. It's a boat. And it's mostly while boating with friends when I've paused and summoned the courage to admit my own life, which has been a series of descents through calm and rough passages, through clear days and rain. Friendship has always been at the center of life for me. I didn't want this trip to be about my fears. Instead I wanted it to be about securing and continuing relationships. I wanted it to give me some insight into the way individual lives all connect in ceaseless flow. I was glad that I'd invited Venable and Steve, two of my closest friends, to join me on this, yet another voyage of watery discovery and enlightenment.

↜ Overnight at Louie's

Venable and I arrived at Louie's land around six at the end of the first day. We pulled our boat out of the current and stashed it above the high water line. When we'd left my backyard that morning, Lawson's Fork wasn't dangerously swollen, but the Pacolet had been rising all afternoon. I looked out at the river, then up at the cloudy late afternoon sky, and thought how it must have been raining harder in the headwaters. All day it had drizzled, and even with a few heavy showers it really wasn't enough to swell the river this much. Securing our boat was essential. We had no idea how much rain would fall overnight.

We'd planned to pitch a tent that first evening on Louie's Pacolet riverfront just like I had a few years earlier on a tune-up trip I'd taken with Steve Patton and my friends Frank Burroughs, Ken Anthony, and his two sons, Dunk and Grady. This time the threat of more rain drove us up the hill. We trudged up the slope to the house, where Venable could make dinner in the kitchen and we'd weather the showers on Louie's porch. Cresting the ridge, I took in Louie and Montana's magical homestead, which I'd always enjoyed visiting. There were groomed trails through the woods, a boat rack, and pens for their goats. As I walked I noticed little concrete statues of elves and saints all along the trail leading out of the woods to the house. They made the property seem enchanted and more appealing, a good stop for our first evening.

The homestead was a cross between *Little House on the Prairie* and the set of *Brigadoon*.

As we left the woods, we saw Louie and Montana's house with its dark siding and a big, screened porch on the front that faced rural Countryside Drive. One of the first things you notice at their place is a small log cabin that Louie had built beside the house; though now the cabin serves only as the tool shed, it gives the homestead a frontier feel, which is only deepened by the domestic turkeys roosting in the oaks around the yard. Just when I thought I'd pegged Louie and Montana as back-to-the-landers, I saw the old, psychedelic graffiti–painted bus off to the side. The vehicle looked just like Further, the bus of Ken Kesey and the Merry Pranksters fame.

We were wet and tired by the time we made it up to the house. Louie showed us the porch where we'd sleep and then disappeared to do a few chores and catch up on the day. Venable found the kitchen right away and focused on cooking.

As we settled in, Venable assembled his world-famous Mexican one-pot dinner in his Dutch oven and placed it inside the electric oven to bake. I assured Venable the meal would taste just as good cooked inside as it would have over coals at the river. Steve, Steve's wife, Penni, and Betsy also drove out to eat with us, and that added a strange twist to our river trip—a dinner party on the first night out.

Later we ate Venable's good Dutch-oven dinner, drank a few more beers, and told stories. I told the story of how on our tune-up trip we'd left our house late and paddled the last two miles to Louie's after sunset and how beavers along both sides of the river slapped their tails as we passed in the dark.

At the end of the evening I walked out to the car with Betsy, Steve, and Penni to say goodbye. I went over the future logistics of the river trip with Steve one more time to make sure all the plans were in place. He was to pick up Venable's Suburban at our house, load on Louie's eighteen-foot Grumman camo-painted aluminum canoe, and meet us in a week at the U.S. 601 bridge on the Congaree at the head of Lake Marion.

"You be careful," Betsy said sweetly as she slipped in the car. She was a little sad and anxious to see me go. "I'd be worried about you if you'd decided to do it alone," she said. "You've got Venable and Steve. I know you'll be safe."

The next morning Louie came down from upstairs where he'd been watching the Weather Channel. "You'll start in the dry but end up in the wet. Down in Georgia it's all green and yellow on the radar, and it's coming our way," he announced.

Louie stepped into the kitchen and started his morning chores. Most days he'd be off early on his landscaping business, and Montana would be off on her thirty-mile commute to Greenville, where she worked as a paralegal in a law office.

"It's nice to hang around the house a little while and relax," Louie said. "I'm hoping I'll retire in three years. I'll do rustic furniture and Montana can do her decorative mirrors." As he talked he fed a baby squirrel with a formula bottle. Venable told Louie how he and his wife, Kim, kept animals on Kim's mother's small farm in Anchorage about ten minutes from their suburban home. They cared for chickens, donkeys, horses, sheep, and until recently, a goose. Louie and Montana's yard was full of chickens and turkeys, and then there were goats out back in a pen. As I watched Louie with the squirrel I thought how Daniel Boone would have understood Louie's relationship to place.

Venable cooked and listened to Louie talk. I stood by and tried to gauge the coming day on the river. "I'm dehydrated from that fifteen-mile day," I said as I filled my water bottle at the sink.

"I don't think it was the river. I think it was those beers last night," Venable said when I complained more vigorously, this time about my headache. He stood at the stove assembling his Dutch oven sausage-and-egg breakfast casserole.

With Venable everything is world famous. This was his "world-famous mountain man breakfast," consisting of potatoes, eggs, sausage, and cheese, cooked as another one-pot meal in the Dutch oven. The night before we'd all indulged in his "world-famous one-pot Mexican dinner" and his "world-famous peach cobbler," and he'd already told us that sometime in our future he would break out his "world-famous Alaskan smoked king salmon." We were scheduled for at least two "treatments" of his "world-famous colon blow," a dried breakfast cereal he developed during his early days of hiking on the Appalachian Trail.

"I know, I know," he said, cracking eggs. "It's an egocentric view of the world."

As I pounded back bottles of water for my headache, I listened to Venable exchange stories with Louie about raising and slaughtering animals. I listened and took notes as they sparred, catching little scraps of the conversation:

Louie: "I raise two hogs a year—one always named Barbeque and one always named Dinner. Farmers around here used to laugh at me. I had a curtain for my pig house, volleyballs in there so they could entertain themselves. They called me the city farmer out here."

Venable: "I've never done a hog that big. I dress wild hogs after I shoot them. They're maybe two hundred pounds."

Louie: "I got a butcher down the road. I throw the hogs on the trailer and he skins them. He's got all the tools—you know, electric saws and grinders."

Venable: "We buy pork shoulders from Costco, but we also make sausage with friends. It helps to have four hands."

Louie: "I used to have twenty-nine hens and I had eggs out the yin-yang, and then Montana moved in. She wanted flowerbeds and shrubs. You know, hens eat shrubs and anything they can in the flowerbeds. So I ended up shooting most of the chickens."

Venable: "Our goose got sick this winter, and I had to shoot him."

After we finished breakfast Louie pulled out a map of the Pacolet River and began talking about his property and the nearby Revolutionary War history. "You know General Daniel Morgan rode right past here," Louie said. "He camped a month across the river before the Battle of Cowpens."

He'd caught my attention. Where, I asked Louie, was the exact location of Morgan's camp? Where was Grindal Shoals? Was it up- or downstream of where we'd taken out the night before?

"They say old man Grindal had a grist mill just upstream of the mouth of Mill Creek," Louie said. "He tied the mill to a tree to keep it from washing downstream in one of the big floods. You'll pass Mill Creek on your paddle today right after you put in."

⌒ Grindal Shoals

Once I went with my friend Terry Ferguson to a history outing dedicated to Grindal Shoals and Morgan's Revolutionary sojourn on the
Pacolet River. The event was held across from Louie's homestead at
a two-hundred-year-old farm on a ridge above the river, land Daniel
Morgan's troops had passed through on the way to Cowpens. As we
walked into the yard, I noticed that there were three dozen cars lined up
in the circular drive for the caravan that morning three miles down to
Grindal Shoals. The Revolution certainly still had its fans. There were
license plates from Vermont, Virginia, Georgia, and North Carolina.

I watched as little groups of old friends met, huddled, and dispersed
all over the yard. As they passed, I listened in. Before we even got
started with the official welcome, they discussed and dismissed a
hundred minute issues: What time of day did Morgan leave Grindal
Shoals? Did he camp on Thickety Creek or farther on? Was it hemor-
rhoids or sciatica, or both, that made Morgan stand up in his saddle?
The questions were posed one after another, and one after another the
answers flew back and forth like volleys on a field of battle.

Terry, an archaeologist, saw I was a little perplexed by the whole
scene. He said, "These are rabid family- and local-history buffs, pas-
sionate in knowing about the past. They're detail oriented. An interesting lot. If you haven't been out with history buffs, you might need

to know that they tend to focus on people. Places like Grindal Shoals are just where the people were at in a given point in time."

"Okay," I told him, "but I look at things in the exact opposite way. Sense of place is more important to me."

"I understand," Terry said. "Just remember: your well-established sense of place is not something they tend to embrace."

As we left the driveway that day and headed down to Grindal Shoals, I marveled at the perfect setting for this old farm. The land fell off around us in every direction. If you could airbrush out the high-tension wires arching over the woods in the distance, you'd find that the picture of rural South Carolina hadn't changed much in two hundred years.

The events at Grindal Shoals are an episode of history that's lost as deep in the past as the shoals themselves. There have been two books associated with the spot, making it one of the most literary landscapes that Venable and I would pass in our float through the upcountry of South Carolina. One book is a slim local history a hundred years old, now found only in a few nearby libraries—*History of Grindal Shoals*, by the Reverend J. D. Bailey. Bailey was a renowned upcountry Baptist preacher and local historian of the Revolution, known mostly for his work about the battles of Kings Mountain and Cowpens. "With a few musty records and lingering traditions, we hope to preserve these remaining fragments, which otherwise must soon be forever lost," he wrote in his brief preface to his Grindal Shoals book.

Bailey's warning about what could be lost has almost come to pass. Now it's mostly Colonial historians, genealogy buffs, and a few nearby neighbors who still remember the spot of land on the Pacolet once known as Grindal Shoals. There is no town to mark the spot, no mill to admire, no dam to demand portage or pause, nothing left but a few hazy facts, old stories, and arguments about Daniel Morgan's camp by those who care to find the spot.

The few historians who have considered it agree that in the eighteenth century the river crossing just downstream from Louie's house was the most important ford in the South Carolina upcountry. By late 1780, when Colonial general Daniel Morgan first camped at Grindal Shoals, a good-sized community as well as two or three gristmills had grown up around the river. What made the place important is that in some ways Morgan's camp was a mini–Valley Forge, though Morgan stayed a much shorter time and was better supplied than his northern counterpart, George Washington.

Before the Revolution, Morgan had run what one local historian calls "an eighteenth century UPS service" in the Carolina backcountry. Morgan's teams of oxen pulled wagons delivering goods from the distant cities. They returned from the Carolina boondocks with deer pelts and barrels of salted "mixed meat," an assortment of whatever the frontiersmen could shoot or kill—plucked songbirds, skinned snakes, possums, raccoons, and fish.

At Grindal Shoals General Morgan gathered his strength and organized his battle plan in late December 1780 and early January 1781, preparing for what would become known as the Battle of Cowpens. On January 14 Morgan received word that elements of the British Army under "Bloody" Banastre Tarleton were approaching. Morgan broke camp the next morning and marched toward Cowpens, about thirty miles distant, where on January 17 he won the battle over Tarleton that many now consider one of the most important of the Revolution.

The second book spotlighting Grindal Shoals, and the one with wider distribution and fame, was *Horse-Shoe Robinson*, by Maryland novelist John P. Kennedy. Kennedy's book, published in 1835, was a best seller and included descriptions of the area around Louie's house. It's said that Kennedy based his descriptions on an actual visit to Grindal Shoals before composition.

The character Horse-Shoe Robinson has been compared to James Fenimore Cooper's Natty Bumppo, another manifestation of the frontier archetype. When Kennedy's novel came out Edgar Allan Poe reviewed it in the *Southern Messenger*. He said, "*Horse-Shoe Robinson* will be eagerly read by all classes of people, and cannot fail to place Mr. Kennedy in a high rank among the writers of this or of any other country."

The novel sold well in the nineteenth century and was read by high school students all over the country well into the twentieth. Now it suffers a fate much like the shoals itself, buried as it is under the sediment of literary history. Very few outside of graduate students in English have heard of either the early novelist Kennedy or his character Horse-Shoe Robinson. It's only when enthusiasts gather that the tiniest details of the novel's plot are discussed, as well as what might be revealed about Louie's neighborhood and its long-ago Revolutionary past.

Later, down at the river, a group of about forty Daniel Morgan devotees walked an ancient rutted path onto the floodplain. I followed them. I hoped they'd lead me to a look at the actual river crossing. As we strolled down the two-track through the cutover woods of a present-day hunt club, there was nothing to suggest the once-thriving village of Grindal Shoals—no vanished tavern, store, houses, grist mills, or law office.

At an intersection, the path to the river forked and picked up gradient. A large pod of pilgrims paused over a rotted pile of tin and wood, and another headed on down the hill. I paused and listened as an older gentleman with sharp piedmont features, dark trousers, white dress shirt, and a large straw hat held court in the shade. "I don't know where you're going," he said to the group headed down the hill. "This is it. You're walking right down the Gravelly Hillock in *Horse-Shoe Robinson*. A natural gravelly hillock it is. Make your way over here. You don't need to go down to the river. See the true ruins of the actual store.

I was here in 1981 with a man whose grandfather ran it, so I know what I'm talking about."

An observer asked: "Was that the store Reverend Bailey talks about in his book?"

"Same one," the man with the straw hat answered. "When I was here in '81 there was still a piece of the old magnolia tree left."

"Where did you say Sally Norris's house was?"

"It was right here. I don't know where they're all going. It's right where Sally Norris's house and Dan Morgan's tent were, though the house wasn't built until 1840."

I passed on by and left the old gentleman holding court. The Order of the Holy Detail is hard to disrupt. I walked down "the gravelly hillock" and through the muddy Grindal Shoals river bottom. I was more interested in seeing the river than searching out the exact route that Morgan and Horse-Shoe Robinson would have taken across the Pacolet.

The old track was lost in a thicket of invasive privet and spindly box elder. As we walked through the bottom, Terry pointed out, "There's probably six to eight feet of recent alluvium between us and any surface those historic figures would have trod."

As we bushwhacked toward the river, I realized that these local historians were exactly the type of ecotourists that Pacolet's mayor, Elaine Harris, hoped would pull her hamlet out of poverty and rural obscurity. Harris had visions of hoards of history buffs descending from far away to track down the route of Dan Morgan from camp to battle. I had to admit, this event had brought them out in good numbers. Maybe Elaine wasn't too far off. The crowd was old though. The average age was close to seventy.

Maybe in my future I too will find comfort, justification, and fulfillment in a simple ramble to the river to hear an old gentleman in a straw hat document the site of a store that closed its doors decades earlier and fell into the weeds. That sort of adventure tourism was a long way from what Betsy and I had in mind when we took our family to Costa Rica. But then again maybe it wasn't. Maybe everyone was playing by the same script now—find your community's uniqueness and exploit it for capital gain. On the trip to Costa Rica something terrible (and unscripted) had happened. My outing down to Grindal Shoals was safer, that's for sure.

By the time Terry and I reached the Pacolet River, I'd abandoned any hope for historical certainty, no matter what the gentleman up the hill in the straw hat had claimed. I'd given up any idea that I might actually pin down the Pacolet's past like a dragonfly at the end of a specimen needle. I looked out at the river's entrenched bed and imagined the old shoals under the weight of history and river mud. "Is this where Morgan crossed?" one of the pilgrims walking with us asked. Who cares? Certainly those up the hill did, but I simply stood for a few minutes and watched the wild river head downstream.

⌐∽ The Wild Pacolet

In *The Things They Carried* author Tim O'Brien tells the story of a platoon in Vietnam. In this collection of stories, the items that the soldiers carry in their backpacks become metaphors of the emotional burdens and hopes that the soldiers bear—some carry love letters, and almost everyone carries photographs, and all carry ammo. "The things they carried were largely determined by necessity," O'Brien writes. "To carry something was to hump it. . . . In its intransitive form, to hump meant to walk, or to march, but it implied burdens far beyond the intransitive."

Paddling trips are not at all like going to war. But the tragedy in Costa Rica was as close as I've ever come to something like combat. Even three months later, off on a great adventure with my friends, I still had lingering emotional stress—had I done anything to prevent the drownings? I could imagine what sort of syndrome might develop after time in the repeated horror of a combat zone.

Venable and I walked down from Louie's place, but most of our gear was in the back of a pickup. I carried one small dry bag dedicated to technology, both low and high, and I hauled it down the hill to keep it safe from the crush of cargo. In the bag there were three steno pads, ten pens and five mechanical pencils, a waterproof camera, my cell phone and extra battery, and my NEO, a full-sized keyboard (with storage for up to five hundred pages) for keeping a running journal of the trip.

I'd seen the NEO in the back of *Writer's Market* and realized right away that it was perfect for a modern-day river voyage like mine. The NEO was made of green molded plastic and ran on four AA batteries. The machine was a typewriter on digital steroids, so durable that they say you can drop it out a window and it keeps on going.

When we arrived at the river we loaded our boat and lowered it down Louie's muddy bank with bow and stern lines. In spite of all our planning, some things we carried were packed above the gunnels, after the allotted cargo space was full. For the second day Venable took his place in the stern, and I took mine in the bow. This was my small way of deferring to Venable's vast experience canoeing, but it was also my way of assuring I could look around a little more and not worry so much about setting the pace and establishing the route downstream. What you lose in power by choosing the bow you gain back in freedom. As they say on the T-shirts in Alaska, "Unless you're the lead dog, the view never changes." So it is for the bow paddler.

We paddled away from shore, and I noticed that the river was a few inches higher than it had been the night before. The river was not running muddy, not yet what I'd call a full-bore flood, but that morning I had my first serious flood anxiety. I felt unsteady in the canoe, as if we had packed it all wrong. The boat felt top-heavy. I know now that I was simply adjusting to hauling the extra weight. Venable's canoe wasn't perfect for our trip, but it was close. His canoe had the blunt nose—called a "bruise water"—of a white-water boat, but that was appropriate because we were expecting white water at several places on the trip. At sixteen feet in length, it had enough cargo space for a trip of ten to fourteen days, also appropriate here, and the hull was a mixed-use shape that would give us some tracking on the long, flat stretches.

We soon passed the site of Grindal Shoals, as imperceptible from the river as it had been from the bank, just as I remembered—no ford, no gristmill, and no road crossing the floodplain and mounting the ridge on the other side. One of Louie's crazy dogs followed us halfway to the Highway 18 bridge, and then, just when we thought we'd have to get him in the canoe with us, he turned and hightailed it home.

As we progressed downstream the rain picked up. From my seat in the bow I looked back at Venable. He had the hood on his camouflage jacket pulled over his head again, and with his wet gray beard he looked like one of those old-time river voyagers committed to the steady task at hand. The rain wasn't really miserable, just wet and persistent. The air wasn't even cold, being late March in South Carolina.

A little later we passed off the first map I'd ripped out of the *Gazetteer* and onto the second. The Highway 18 bridge was the boundary. The event was a ceremonial passing that only I noted, as the maps were secured against the rain in the dry bag.

About midday we passed Skull Shoals' concrete landing. In spite of its ominous name, there were no shoals and definitely no skull. The rocks are now lost under layers of sediment, and whatever story or event gave the place its name hasn't been recorded in the local history.

Here in the spring of 1880 G. W. Garner, his brother S.L., and a black servant set out on a three-week pleasure trip to the ocean. They left Skull Shoals in a plank boat eighteen feet long and four feet wide and worked by oars. "Quietly they floated down the Pacolet to the Broad at Pinckney Ferry by easy stages to Columbia," the local newspaper reported. Along the way they ate squirrels and ducks, and every night when they came to a good spot they camped. After spending a few days in Columbia they continued on down the Congaree and there, done in by the "interminable swamps," their black companion came to the conclusion that he was "about as far from the hills [at] Skull Shoals as he desired to be." He took the next train home. The brothers continued to the coast. Sometimes they didn't see a house or boat for days, and all they saw was "forests and swamps . . . on all sides." Arriving in Georgetown, the Garners took in the old city for a few days, then they sold the boat for the original cost of the lumber and took a train home.

Upstream from Skull Shoals is where the Wofford College River Voyageurs put in early in January 1969, under direction of Doc Stober. They'd noted in their journal how much trash there was on the river: "Litter and waste floated down the Pacolet River and lined the shores. Everything from clothesbaskets and plastic balls to tractor tires and beer bottles was seen, making the muddy waters of the Pacolet seem bleak. The ultimate in waste that was observed was raw sewage." The Clean Water Act of 1972 had improved our passage a great deal. The river felt alive and healthy. There was nothing bleak about it except the weather. The sewage was now treated, and the Industrial Revolution had mostly left the Upcountry and migrated to China, leaving our river to recover.

Almost forty years earlier Doc Stober's River Voyageurs had observed "a few species of birds—thrush, cardinal, robin in small numbers" and "a few summer ducks, cranes, blue herons, and canvas backs." Along the shore there were "cattle grazing on pasture land and in the wooded areas." Our second day on the river we saw nesting Canada geese, several osprey, deer, numerous beaver dams, and a turkey that flew over the river.

We stopped on a sandbar and ate lunch. We had a good one—tortillas, peanut butter and honey, a Gala apple from halfway around the world, and a Panera bakery cookie. I'd been holding out on Venable about the special cookies I'd purchased, one a piece each of our eight days, and when I pulled out those extravagant oatmeal raisin monsters, Venable's mood brightened considerably. Venable's wife had encouraged him to use this trip to the wilderness to lose a few pounds from his imposing presence. He had dutifully planned the menu accordingly. With the advent of the cookies into the daily mix it now seemed possible the trip might contain enough calories to get Venable downstream.

We were back on the river soon after lunch. Cruising through the Pacolet's numerous bends, Venable commented on how surprised he was that so many power lines crossed the river, and how with the traffic noise the highways seemed so close sometimes, and how the replacement bridges were being rebuilt higher and higher back where the highway crossed Skull Shoals. Venable also noted the frequency of pileated woodpeckers in the spring woods, the beauty of the redbud in bloom, and the alternating stands of natural hardwoods (with a few trees already leafed out) and planted pines along the shore.

I'd also spotted tree stands along the river all morning. When I mentioned this to Venable he didn't wax philosophically about hunting or hunt clubs. He assessed their placement as to view, shooting lanes, likely paths for the approach for deer, and so on. "I get the feeling that every landowner along this river has pressed standing timber and clear-cut bottom into the service of hunting," I said, a little disgusted.

"Southerners have always hunted. It's in our cultural blood," Venable noted.

I had to agree. Land and game (and the hunting of it) are traditional elements of our highly touted sense of place. It's even argued by some, like the late historian Jack Temple Kirby, that the sense of a southern "commons" lingered longer down here than any other region. Southerners have always had access to the land around them, and they've used it for hunting and gathering. They crossed neighboring land on horseback and foot. Even though they didn't own it, they saw nearby parcels of forest and fields as a commons they could utilize.

"If Kirby is right, it might explain why southern hunters are often trespassers and poachers to this day," Venable said.

As the population of upcountry South Carolina has grown, so has the abundance of deer and turkey. And so has pressure from poachers and hunters who trespass on land owned by the absentees. Upcountry deer hunting is not the ritual described in Faulkner's "The Bear," where the old-money blue bloods retreat into the endless ancient hardwood bottoms to renew their ties with their ancestral land. Now hunting is a huge industrial recreation, and hunting land is a playground, not a wilderness commanding respect.

If landowners have not developed their own hunt camps, complete with lodges, fire pits, and butcher stands, then they've leased the hunting rights to cousins or acquaintances. It's an easy paycheck. You keep the land, and someone else is responsible for keeping the gates up. The tree stands we saw everywhere along the Pacolet were recurrent signs of this usage. They make our watery commons not so inviting to paddle during the few months of deer season.

But why so many hunt clubs? There are many people who want to hunt, and the land now has become mostly real estate. Litigation has also become a worry for every landowner. There are high-powered rifles (lots of them) in the woods now, so it's more important than ever that landowners control access, especially during hunting season.

Alas, the commons is forever gone.

A friend once told me how his grandfather owned a few hundred acres on a local Spartanburg County creek. The land came down in his family, and he really didn't want to sell it, though subdivisions were pressing in from two sides. He hadn't cut the timber off it either, though chip mills sent him regular letters. He'd never leased it out as hunting land, but a few years ago he gave informal hunting permission to a local bow hunter, with the understanding that he and he alone would hunt on it. But soon this man had invited a dozen of his favorite friends to join him, and they weren't all bow hunters. High-powered rifles were their weapons of choice.

The bow hunter and his buddies weren't the only ones who saw the land as their personal commons. Recreation in the rural South often means dirt bikes and four-wheelers. After the gates went up and the property was posted, one homeowner from the nearby subdivision came to my friend's grandfather and asked, "Where are my kids supposed to ride their dirt bikes now?" There are no simple answers to the problem of contemporary recreation in the South.

When I aired my meditations on hunting land, Venable, as always, complicated my quick conclusions. He saw the hunting property we were passing as an insider. "I can't help but see where the turkeys might roost," he said, "where the deer might look for mast. I don't carry the negative charge you do in every observation of land put to use by local boys for hunting."

I thought for a moment about what Venable had said and had to admit that the concept of hunting land does have a negative charge for me. "You've got to remember I'm a public parks and wilderness guy," I explained. "More John Muir than Teddy Roosevelt. I'd like to transform private hunting land into federally designated wilderness. As I pass this land I think 'rewild.' I'm using the imminent domain of my literary imagination to cancel the deeds and the hunting leases and turn Union County into Piedmont National Park."

"Good luck, Mr. Muir," Venable said.

This talk of hunting, hunting land, and wildness recalled a long-standing discussion we'd had about Alaska and the portrayal of "wildness" in the book and film *Into the Wild*. The subject was one we always seemed to return to, and sometimes we lingered on its elements longer than other issues. I'd made it clear to Venable in the past that I appreciated the way both Jon Krakauer's book and Sean Penn's film had made Alaska into the ultimate wilderness destination and Romantic rest stop for dreamers like the book and film's hero, Christopher McCandless. My fascination with *Into the Wild* was one aspect of my thinking that Venable could never understand.

Most people know the story, one of a sloppy search for adolescent freedom and transcendence, its rewards and risks. It's based on real events documented by Krakauer's best-selling book. You might have at least heard the plot line by now: Soon after graduating from Emory University, privileged McCandless gives his $24,000 trust fund to Oxfam, drives west, leaves his old Toyota abandoned off-road, burns his last few hundred dollars, bums around channeling the literary ghosts of Jack Kerouac and Jack London, paddles the Colorado River, and finally heads north, "into the wild," to discover the meaning of life among big mountains.

After that, things turn both good and bad. McCandless (who took the road name Alexander Supertramp) screws up and can't ford a glacial river to walk out when he's ready to return to civilization. He tries foraging for food, reads the field guide wrong, and eats a wild plant that kills him. Chris/Alex dies in an old city bus somebody's hauled into the woods for a hunting cabin. In the end he's staring at the sky looking for a transcendence that he's sought since childhood, in both literature and experience. Like so many careless artists and searchers, he dies in his early twenties. Moose hunters later find his body, and his sister flies his ashes home.

I always tell my beginning literature students not to neglect pondering the title, and in this case it's a big fat finger pointing to the story's theme. Examining wildness is the point of this film, and the search for it is something you usually see Hollywood directors exploring in cities through murder, greed, graft, sex, and swindling, good old American antivalues.

"McCandless was an idiot," Venable said, paddling along. "He had no plan, no back up or safety net. He had no extra food or knowledge of snow or of when the ice would melt. He was an idiot because he wasn't prepared. And besides, Jon Krakauer got the cause of death wrong, and forensics and botanists later proved that the plant Krakauer said killed McCandless wasn't poison. So Krakauer's an idiot for portraying him as heroic."

"On a personal level I see my own idealistic wasted youth splattered across the screen in vivid colors each time I watch the film."

"McCandless might have been able to read Tolstoy, but he had serious trouble with his field guide to edible plants. After college, he made an A on the Enlightenment, but he failed natural history. His final grade is C– average. His mistakes killed him."

"Hello, my name is John, and I too wanted at twenty-two to walk into the wild and act like I had no past or future."

"I can't believe you're *that* stupid," Venable said. "You're no idiot like McCandless."

In spite of Venable's protests, *Into the Wild* makes me think about all the bullets I've dodged. We can all decide whether McCandless is an idiot or a hero. I see him as both, maybe a necessary tension in life. I looked down in the bow of the canoe and saw the yellow bag containing the throw rope. Was I an idiot for my lack of preparation in Costa Rica? I didn't have a throw rope with me. I'd trusted the outfitter would provide what support was needed. I had no safety net. I'd simply been along for the ride. When I was standing on the beach and Jeremy and the others came floating by after the accident, I could have pulled them to shore with a rope if I'd had one. Instead I had simply watched the scene unfold like a movie. I looked back downstream. The steady rain scored the moving surface of the river with a thousand small collisions.

"Well, I'm glad I didn't walk quite as far in as McCandless," I finally admitted after a period of silence. "I'm glad I didn't end up dead in that bus in Alaska. But I think I could have. I like it when a film shows another possible me that I somehow bypassed. I've been inches away a dozen times from being McCandless. But I never went that far into the wild."

Venable wasn't buying it. "Be prepared. Many of us learned that when we were ten years old."

◝ Confluence

Five hours below Louie's we left the Pacolet River behind and floated into the Broad. The larger river's expanse surprised me a little. After two days of paddling I was used to the intimate confines of another order of stream. At the confluence of Lawson's Fork and the Pacolet the width of the stream had tripled from thirty to ninety feet. At the confluence of the Pacolet and the Broad it tripled again. We were now looking at a truly broad river. "It's definitely wider than forty yards, the maximum distance I'd shoot a turkey," Venable said when I asked him to estimate the width.

The idea of stream order or hierarchy was officially proposed in 1952 by a geosciences professor at Columbia University named Arthur Newell Strahler. He proposed that streams could be classified in sizes ranging from the smallest first-order streams all the way to the largest twelfth-order streams. In Strahler's system smaller streams always feed larger streams, and the smaller streams usually have steeper slopes. In this system the Mississippi River is a tenth-order stream, and the Amazon, the largest river in the world, is a twelfth-order stream.

I thought back over our two days and decided that my home stream, Lawson's Fork, was probably a third-order stream with a small network of tributaries, and the Pacolet and Broad would probably be classified as fourth- and fifth-order streams. By the time I'd reached the coast

I'd probably be looking at about an eighth-order stream in the lower reaches of the Santee.

Leaving the Pacolet and moving into the current of the Broad, we had paddled across the ancient line of demarcation between the Cherokee Nation to the west and the Catawba Nation to the east. "Eswau Huppeday," Venable said with great flair and some dramatic humor as we let the river carry us along. He was repeating the Catawba name for the Broad River he'd learned from reading Henry Savage's book about the river system. "Eswau Huppeday, the Boundary River," he said.

The Broad River upstream from the Pacolet's confluence is a South Carolina State Scenic River, and the landowners take great pride in its rural setting and long, lonely reaches of river. With the egos and power that have been brought to bear on this river system since the early nineteenth century it's almost a miracle that any of the river has survived undammed.

In *River of the Carolinas* Henry Savage describes how in 1904 James Buchanan "Buck" Duke, the tobacco heir, and Walker Gill Wylie met in New York when Wylie treated Duke for a foot problem. After the transplanted southerners were brought together over a house call, the rivers of the Carolinas would never be the same. Both men, come to find out, were experimenting with waterpower for the generation of electricity.

Earlier, Duke had built a small plant on the Raritan River in New Jersey. Back home, in the watershed of the Catawba (part of the Santee watershed we were paddling), Wylie had commissioned a young engineer named William States Lee to build a hydroelectric plant on his plantation, near Chester, South Carolina.

Returning to treat Duke day after day, Wylie told him of a dream that he and the engineer had shared—that the entire Catawba-Broad-Wateree system would one day be a vast hydro-lake from mountains to coastal plain, powering factories and homes all across the Carolinas.

In 1904, with funding from Duke and Wylie, Lee formed the Southern Power Company (now Duke Energy), the pioneer hydro-electric system in the world at the time. In two decades the Catawba-Wateree would became the most developed power river in the United States, a boast that the Carolinas could make until the Tennessee Valley Authority of the 1930s.

Great Falls on the Catawba was their first joint project. Another one at Rocky Creek followed that dam. "Others undertaken in that first busy decade of the mammoth plan were [dams at] . . . Lookout Shoals . . . Fishing Creek . . . Wateree near Camden," Savage writes, "and a one-hundred-and-thirty-five-foot one up against the mountains near Morganton."

We paddled into the current of the Broad, and Venable said how he was surprised by the serenity and isolation: "Out west this would be unheard of. All the big river junctions have towns in their crotches."

I told him it hadn't always been so wild. We were passing the site of the vanished Colonial town of Pinckneyville on the south bank. Like Grindal Shoals upstream, there was nothing left for us to see from the river but trees and a muddy bank. The site is now yet another hunt club.

In 1791 the Pinckney District was created in the Carolina backcountry, an area comprising what is now Union, Spartanburg, York, Chester, and Cherokee counties. A spot at the confluence of the Pacolet and Broad rivers was selected as the site of the new courthouse. The location had been an important trading post since 1752, and there were high hopes for the new settlement. Soon after the courthouse and jail were constructed a flood drowned the infant city. As one historian reported it, in 1792 "a tremendous freshet poured down upon the two rivers, and [the rivers] overflowed all that had been done, all in a promiscuous ruin."

The next year the South Carolina upcountry pioneers rebuilt Pinckneyville farther from the river. For a few decades stagecoaches ran to the town from the more "civilized" midlands, where Columbia was already thriving. They crossed the Broad River at Pinckney Ferry a short distance downstream from the confluence with the Pacolet. There was a log school building, but strangely enough, no church. A Charleston surveyor laid out streets and gave them names with plenty of pretense: Meeting, Broad, Tradd, names taken directly from the roster of streets in low-country Charleston. It's said the town was named for a low-country hero as well, Charles Cotesworth Pinckney, a Revolutionary War veteran and one of South Carolina's delegates to the Constitutional Convention. One of the oddest legends about the vanished community we were passing was that Congress considered it as the location for the nation's military academy in the early nineteenth century.

Pinckneyville died when the railroad chose to go to what would become the town of Union instead. Now it has no Main Street, no separate zip code, not even a minimart. The vanished town adds nothing to Union County's shrinking economic base. All that's left in Pinckneyville are two brick walls of the collapsed jail on a scrubby clear-cut ridge above the Pacolet River. The ghost town is South Carolina's poster child for lost opportunity. Beware city planners: prosperity and progress are one bad break away from vanishing. If things go one way or another any town could pass into history; all that could be left of a community is a pile of bricks and a few notes filed away in the cabinets of old men with straw hats.

Just down the Broad River on the right bank was a concrete boat dock that belonged to a friend of mine from the buildings and grounds department at Wofford College. My friend was part of a group that leased a hunt club there, and he fished as often as possible on the river. The Broad is shoally in that stretch, and my friend often ran his shallow-draft aluminum Everglades-style airboat up and down when he fished. The airboat must have created an odd scene—and a deafening racket—when he cranked the airplane propeller and hauled around the river from fishing hole to fishing hole.

"So you want to 'rewild' it all?" Venable said as I told him about the airboat and the fishing. "You want to return Eswau Huppeday to pristine wilderness and throw your buddy out of his weekend paradise?"

"As King of the Upcountry I decree that Tim and his airboat can stay," I said, sweeping my paddle in the direction of my friend's boat landing. "He has a life-lease from this moment on."

"Ah, the complexities of civilization," Venable said, bringing his sarcasm to closure.

⌒ *Night on Goat Island*

After we paddled another half-mile, Goat Island rose up in the middle
of the river. The island was bigger than a cabin cruiser but smaller than
a yacht. On the upriver end the island's sand prow is a dozen feet high
and thick with river birch and sycamore. On the downriver end a thin
line of sycamores had taken root on a low sandbar. Farther down the
river, deposits of white sand had built up and spread out in flats and
fleecy dunes.

A hard and steady rain fell as we pulled ashore on the sandbar.
Venable and I set to work rigging the big silver tarp. There were white
lines trailing from each corner and a long section of line coiled for the
centerline. Venable was an expert at tarp-rigging from his Alaska adventures. "A steady rain like this is why you bring a tarp. It's the first
thing you put up," he said as he stretched out the lines and attached
one to a small sycamore. "And it's the last thing you strike before you
get in the canoe."

In a few minutes the tarp was almost up. The high end of the centerline was tied to the sycamore and the low end to our beached canoe.
Venable adjusted the tension on the lines by slipping a canoe paddle
underneath. He used several of his Boy Scout knots to secure it. By the
time he was finished he had the big silver flap positioned to shed the
deluge to either side.

After Venable had tied the last line, we stashed the gear from our canoe underneath the tarp. The rain was falling harder by the time I climbed under with my NEO and unrolled my collapsible Crazy Creek camp chair in the sand. I was glad Venable had made such a big deal out of bringing the tarp. I surveyed our good gear—the best dry bags money could buy. We had dry clothes and easily stored cooking equipment. Sitting under Venable's tarp I relaxed a little, but I felt a little tension too. A river trip boils everything down to the basics—paddle, pitch camp, cook, sleep, clean, strike camp, paddle. But what adjustments have to be made if one of your basics is writing? Where did I fit it in? On a river trip the old adage of "Do the hard stuff first" comes through loud and clear, but I'll admit it was only with reluctance that I crawled out from under the tarp to pitch camp.

Venable had wandered off to call Kim in Alaska. He found a spot of cell phone service on the top of the sand ridge.

"Now isn't that the modern world?" he said when he crawled back under the tarp. "I'm calling Alaska from Goat Island and Kim says, 'Kirk's on the other line calling from Istanbul. Can I call you back later?'"

I took notes and began to think about Henry Savage. There I was, camped on an island he'd never seen, watching the river flow and the night fall. How different were we, river writer Henry Savage and I? His concerns and mine seemed worlds apart at that moment. We were separated in time by half a century, and our voices were shaped by the different periods in which we wrote. Maybe it never occurred to Savage to write a first-person narrative about his beloved Santee River system. Maybe the demands of the Rivers of America series didn't allow it. In three hundred pages Savage never drives to the headwaters of the Broad, Catawba, or Saluda and drops a canoe in a living flowing stream like we had done two days before.

I wanted immediacy, vividness, personal history, first-person revelry, dialogue with real characters, natural history, unexpected encounters with the river. He'd wanted objectivity, depth of human culture and history, authority of research. Did he ever find a place in his lifetime of narratives for a river companion like the one I was watching on the island?

Maybe I wasn't looking for the wrong river when I opened up *River of the Carolinas* after all. Maybe Henry Savage's mythic narrative about the human history that a watershed can hold is instructive for my contemporary nature writer's voice. "The river remembers!" Savage says in his final paragraph. "But life, like the river, flows on and man, obsessed with immortality, looks forward into an uncertain future."

"I am the chronicler of that future," I wrote in my journal, "and the river is still here. I am paddling both Henry's river and mine." I vowed to update Savage's narrative to my own early twenty-first-century style. Maybe someday my book would take its place alongside Henry's on a dusty library shelf, to be picked up in fifty years by another generation's river voyager with yet another perspective and style.

Lockhart Portage

The morning of the third day we paddled three slack water miles from Goat Island to Lockhart. We left the island at eleven, and it had rained the entire morning without ceasing. The weather had tamped down our spirits.

Just downstream from the island at the remote, former cotton mill town of Lockhart the Broad River falls forty-seven feet in two miles. We approached the dam and took out at a landing Lockhart Power had provided on river right. After we landed I looked downstream. Half the gradient was covered up under the impoundment behind the dam, but downstream what was visible of the shoals was impressive. Connected to the dam on river right I could see the long canal once used for power production, and below that, two dozen saltbox mill houses. From previous river trips I knew the old powerhouse was out of sight in the distance at the lower end of the shoals. That's where we could put the canoe back in the river.

On relicensing a few years before, Lockhart Power agreed to provide a portage service for recreational paddlers on the Broad River, so at the take-out, I picked up a phone and called for a shuttle, a nice luxury.

Lockhart has a long history going back to the early nineteenth century. An extensive lock system was designed in the 1820s for moving barges around the Broad River's formidable shoals. Below the dam and the village were the abandoned ruins of three locks and a canal in the woods along the southern shore. In 1994 the mill closed, putting 231 out of work. A few years later the mill was demolished. Lockhart was the smallest town in South Carolina, with only thirty-nine citizens reported in the 2000 census. Eventually even the local high school had closed.

"The little town that time forgot," Betsy had called Lockhart once when we were driving through on Highway 9. Looking down into Lockhart you look into South Carolina's almost forgotten river and textile past. Lockhart Power still diverts the river to generate electricity, but that's the Broad River's only connection to the community now, save for a few fishermen and canoeists like us. The nearest Wal-Mart was fifteen miles away, a good indication of how isolated it felt down there.

By 1820 the Broad River system had been opened up to barge traffic all the way to Lockhart. A canal at Lockhart would open up the Pacolet and upper tributaries of the Broad to barge traffic as well, and so the canal there was built on the west side of the river between 1820 and 1823. The original canal consisted of six granite locks and a guard lock at the upriver end. In its heyday almost two thousand bales of upcountry cotton passed downriver through the locks every year. The old canal was closed to barge traffic in 1849, but historians believe that, soon after, the canal was enlarged and a new cut was made into the river above the old entrance. There wasn't a cotton mill at Lockhart Shoals (as it was first known) until 1893, but an early atlas shows a sawmill there.

Paddlers who had preceded us had experienced all sorts of different portages in Lockhart. There was probably some sort of dam across the river in 1880 when the Garner brothers came through. And Doc Stober's River Voyageurs had set up a portage of the Lockhart dam before they left Pacolet in 1969. They'd launched nine canoe teams consisting of seventeen students and Stober. They were transported in several trucks from Lockhart to their next put-in spot ten miles downstream, below Neal Shoals dam. Their journal chronicles how two of the River Voyageurs had a project concerning the canals on the Santee River System, and so they were interested in the locks at Lockhart. Before they shuttled downstream they asked two old men at a country store if they knew anything about the Lockhart Canal. "One man told us the old canal ran the same course as the new one but it was smaller," the authors of the journal entry reported. They told them that before water was released you could see remnants of the old walls in the new channel. The old men also told the Wofford boys to look in the woods below the powerhouse and they'd find other remnants of the original canal. On their search the boys found three sets of granite locks and the overgrown canal. "The river seemed much too far away from our find to have been part of the canal, but the years have done much to alter the course of the river," their report reads.

In 1981, when Steve Patton came through, there was no phone for shuttle service, but he caught a ride around the dam with a man from the power company. He left Steve near the powerhouse, and that night (Steve's first on the river) Steve paddled a little downstream and set up camp near where water from the old canal reentered the river. He made a fire that night and noted in his journal that "driftwood makes a smoky fire."

When David Taylor came through Lockhart on his 1999 paddle, he found the power company office, and two men there offered him a ride. He loaded his kayak in their truck. They gave him a Gatorade and generously took him to the Lockhart Zippy Mart for a cheeseburger.

On our tune-up trip to Columbia in 2006 we'd surprised the power company's portage driver by showing up with four canoes and eight paddlers. He'd arrived in a tiny truck, and he took one look at our canoes and mountain of gear and returned an hour later with a dump truck.

This time Robert Ellis from Lockhart Power Company arrived in his full-sized pickup a few minutes after we called. He was a tall man in a Lockhart Power cap, a camouflage hunting jacket, and clean pressed chinos. As we covered the mile from take-out to put-in we asked about the canoe traffic.

Ellis said that one big school group had come through a week before, but there really weren't that many. "Maybe two or three a month."

In a small-world moment we found out Ellis had married a woman from Spartanburg.

"Her family owns all that land on the left bank of the Pacolet right before you get to the Broad," he explained when we told him we'd paddled down the day before.

Talking about Ellis's wife's family's land led to Venable's discovery they had something in common—turkey hunting—and so they talked about turkey season, which opened the next day. "A day later and I wouldn't have been here to shuttle you, that's for sure," Ellis said.

As he drove, Ellis talked about his personal history with Lockhart. He'd worked there for forty years and expressed sadness about what had happened to the village since the mill closed in 1994. "This used to be a good little town," he said as we drove past the big empty lot where the mill had stood. "Not much left of it now."

Generation of power is the only industry to survive in Lockhart. Lockhart Power maintains a small, highly efficient operation by diverting the river through an expanded version of the old barge canal. Ellis was proud of the company and told us a little about it. Established in 1912 the company provides electric service to about seven thousand customers through ninety miles of transmission line, he said. Its rates are among the lowest in South Carolina.

Ellis dropped us in the powerhouse parking lot, and we moved our gear down the portage trail to where we would put back in. Venable shouldered the canoe again, and I loaded up with the dry bags. We hauled the gear down the gravel trail; the rain didn't make the conclusion of the portage any easier. Once I'd dropped my first load of gear by the riverside I looked back upstream at a half-mile of piedmont shoals. The passage was rocky and shallow since most of the water of the Broad had been diverted into the canal. It would have been an ordeal to descend in the canoe. It was obvious what an obstacle the stretch would have presented for early commerce. The truck-based shuttle had provided a much more appealing portage.

The Broad River has six power dams on its main stem. Three were up stream of where we joined the Broad. Lockhart was the first we saw. We still had Neal Shoals and Parr Shoals Reservoir to go. Built mostly in the 1920s and 1930s, each dam produced power by taking advantage of the river's drop between the mountains and Columbia. But these dams also create a series of linear storage basins—more like a wide river than a lake. Other than Parr Shoals Dam two days downstream, these aren't dams that inundate large swaths of bottomland.

Was the trade worth it, the drop and surge of a wild river sacrificed for this little power operation? The question had been settled long ago with the public, so maybe it was one that I shouldn't put too much time into considering. It's one thing to contemplate removing abandoned dams higher up on Lawson's Fork, but to think about removing a large dam like Lockhart on the main stem of a river seems almost revolutionary. I could do all the Edward Abbey dreaming I liked, but the dams weren't coming out no matter what I thought.

"Not a bad way to make power," Venable said when he saw me looking upstream at the shoals and then over at the elegant, 1920s-era brick powerhouse. "It puts clean water back in the river."

As we walked down from the powerhouse we passed two oddball

local boys out in the rain, fishing in the canal on their day off. The only rain gear they'd brought along were the caps they wore. They had on soaked-through sleeveless tees. They seemed friendly enough, and they smiled as we passed.

"How's the fishing?" Venable asked.

The two boys didn't seem surprised to see us out in the rain. "Y'all fishing too?"

Venable slowed down and dropped the dry bags he was carrying. "We're canoeing down to Wood's Ferry," he explained.

"You be careful on that river," one boy said. "They say there's big storms coming up this evening. You better get down there before they hit."

"We'll be careful."

"Hey, if y'all's fishing," the other boy added, "they's good smallmouth all up and down through there. I wouldn't waste it. I'd drop a line."

We portaged our gear and walked back up in the pouring rain. A loading dock under a corner of the old powerhouse kept us dry and offered a little bit of refuge as we ate our lunch. We tried our cell phones but neither worked. Venable unwrapped his world-famous smoked king salmon and passed me a golden brown slab. I ate the fish and considered how fortunate I was for Venable's hand-smoked salmon from Alaska to end up on the side of the Broad River in South Carolina. Early river voyagers would have smoked and eaten river fish, and so I fell in line with that long tradition. When I finished I licked the sweet oil off my fingers as the last morsel disappeared.

After we'd savored the fish, I broke out the big cookies and said it was hard to believe it was already day three and that we were on the long straight stretch of the Broad River that would lead us to Columbia. "The boundary river," I said, recalling Venable's earlier evocation of the Catawba's river. "We're right on the edge."

ᴄ᷍ᴐ Wood's Ferry Campground

We left Lockhart and the postindustrial world farther and farther behind. What used to be "a good little town" was now a place slowly disappearing from the map. Contemporary economics was rewilding the piedmont. Lockhart was far from the interstate, far from anything resembling a city. As we paddled in driving rain I wondered whether the town would exist as something other than a power station in a hundred years. The river below Lockhart had the real feel of the wild South returning. We paddled through thick bottomland forest and the current picked up.

Early in the afternoon it felt like I was finally entering the part of the trip I'd looked forward to all these years. I was with a good friend, and the two of us were alone on a big rising river. The day looked as if it offered potential for real wildness. Until we reached Columbia on the afternoon of day five, we'd see few houses. There were scant road crossings from Lockhart on down either. When I'd showed Betsy the maps for the trips, she'd looked at the passages on days four and five and said, "That's desolate South Carolina backcountry down through there."

Not far downstream from Lockhart there's a Mississippian period American Indian mound where Turkey Creek comes into the Broad River. The mound, used for burial and as a platform for a lodge, was listed on the National Register of Historic Places in 1972. It's located on private property. When I'd paddled through in 2006, a friend of mine who hunts the property had tied a piece of orange flagging tape to a tree hanging out over the river so we'd know where to enter the woods to get a look at the mound. I'd walked fifty yards into the woods to the site. It was protected from view by a margin of stunted floodplain trees and planted pines. The ten-foot mound itself had been looted many times and was pocked with the holes of relic hunters. In spite of a hundred years of violation and tree farming, the place was still magical, an aboriginal dirt mound rising mysteriously from the surrounding flat floodplain. As we walked toward the mound, it was easy to fill the river bottom with green corn and hear the chants of the priests.

As Venable and I passed, we didn't see any sign of the flagging tape from the previous trip. It was raining so hard we decided not to stop. As we reached the confluence of Turkey Creek and the Broad, I looked deep into the woods toward where I knew the mound rose from the floodplain, but I couldn't see anything through the gloom and torrents of rain.

We paddled for three more hours through some of the hardest rain I'd ever experienced. The rain came down in sheets and battered the surface of the river. Drifts of cloud floated between the low, gunmetal sky and our canoe. I kept my head down and my hood pulled tight. I simply paddled. Venable kept us aimed downstream with his powerful J-stroke.

After we'd been quiet a long time, paddling through the driving rain, I made the mistake of articulating my reverie about wildness out loud: "I'm glad we'll be in the wilderness the next two nights."

"Wilderness?" Venable spit the word out as if he'd just swallowed a bug. "If something went bad you could walk a mile or two in any direction and be on a road."

Being from Alaska Venable certainly knew about wilderness. For him the Broad River below Lockhart in upcountry South Carolina was no wilderness. But wasn't it all perspective? Despite what Venable said, the river was plenty wild enough for me.

Below the site of the Turkey Creek Mound, we began paddling through a long stretch of Sumter National Forest. The 340,000-acre forest is one of only two federal forests in South Carolina, and I'd be paddling through the other, Francis Marion National Forest, on my final push to the sea on days ten and eleven. Named for Thomas Sumter, a leader of rebel partisan forces in the South Carolina piedmont during the American Revolution, Sumter National Forest was established by Franklin D. Roosevelt in July 1936. The lands that became the forest were, during the Depression, eroding farm fields, gullies, and logged-out barrens. Upon the founding of the national forest, the U.S. government began the process of controlling erosion, and timber production began. Today, the forest is known for many backcountry activities—horseback and mountain bike trail riding, hiking, hunting, and fishing.

We'd be paddling through the Sumter National Forest for a day and a half. On the right bank a narrow strip of Chester County buffered the river from private land, but on the left bank fifty-five thousand acres of the forest took up about a quarter of Union County's land, a percentage of government ownership approaching Western proportions. I'd been told that the forest made for good deer and turkey hunting and that hunters were about the only industry Union could still count on.

We floated along surrounded by public land, and I felt like singing Woody Guthrie's song—"This land is your land / This land is my land." The river was a commons, and these large stretches of national forest can, if managed properly, function as a receptacle for our shared heritage.

As we paddled through the South Carolina backcountry, I was happy that our government had shown the foresight to preserve and protect large swaths of Union County from private interests. I knew not all South Carolinians felt the same way about public land. The idea of public land had been under siege the last few decades, particularly during the Reagan and Bush years. A libertarian spirit pervaded the South Carolina backcountry. Government, as Reagan stated in the early 1980s, was seen as the enemy: "Man is not free unless government is limited," he said, and, "Concentrated power has always been the enemy of liberty." As I floated through Sumter National Forest, I was glad that the long arm of government had reached as far as the South Carolina backcountry. I preferred a national management plan for our shared space, not the individual dreams of local fishermen like we had met at Lockhart.

By midafternoon we pulled into Wood's Ferry, a Forest Service campground with access to the river. Wood's Ferry is fifteen miles from the nearest town, even closer to Betsy's middle of nowhere than Lockhart. The river's the only reason anybody would go there, and only three activities await you: fishing, resting, and troublemaking.

As we floated up, I noticed the campground was empty. When I'd come through with my friends in the spring of 2006, Wood's Ferry had been crowded with campers. Late that night one wild local boy had ridden his white horse around the campground like Horse-Shoe Robinson with the Tories chasing him. We hadn't slept much that night.

Venable and I hauled the canoe up the concrete boat ramp and unloaded in the pouring rain. The parking lot was already flooded, and large gray puddles had formed in the sparse, pot-holed gravel. From the looks of things it seemed the libertarians had won. The campground could have used some government work. We wondered whether we were too early for spring-cleaning or whether the budget had been cut. The blooming pink of the understory redbuds was the only color brightening the scene. We had the campground all to ourselves in the rain.

We commandeered a picnic shelter right next to the most beautiful redbud in bloom and strung our wet clothes up on the rope from Venable's yellow throw bag. We spread wet raincoats out over two tables. Venable reminded me of what the two fishermen back at Lockhart had told us: Expect severe storms that night.

"We should wait to set the tent up," he said, so we sat in the middle of the open-sided shelter as the hard vertical rain whipped in from outside. Both dead tired, we sat and simply watched the rain like bored old men tuned into a TV show.

On that earlier trip in 2006 a friend named Roger Lindsay had visited us at Wood's Ferry to give a full-fledged primitive technology demonstration in the parking lot. A master flint knapper, he'd opened the hatch on his minivan and laid out his re-created wares on a picnic table—beautifully crafted chert points, dart throwers (atlatls), darts for the atlatls made from river cane, and perfectly balanced bows and arrows.

In the parking lot we watched as Roger performed the two-hop dance of native hunters ten thousand years ago. He launched an atlatl spear. The projectile gyrated strangely in the air like a corkscrew but then stuck in the cleared ground between where we stood and the river. Roger said he'd hunted turkeys successfully with the atlatl once or twice. He'd even come in second in a senior atlatl tournament.

I sat looking out into the rain and thought of Roger and the human need for weapons. A friend had asked if I planned to be armed on my paddle to the sea. I said I hadn't thought about it, that I'd never carried a gun on a river trip before, and so why should I start now? He said he couldn't imagine paddling through backcountry South Carolina without firearms. "It just doesn't seem southern."

As we had prepared to paddle to the sea, Venable had asked if I wanted him to bring a gun along. He had access to plenty of them at his brother's house in Georgia. "I want to go without one," I had said. "Remember, I'm one of those tree-hugging river rats who doesn't own or carry a gun. I've never had a hint of anxiety out in the wild that wasn't human induced."

"Exactly why so many carry guns," Venable said. "To protect ourselves from our own species."

A truck pulled into the parking lot and slowed to a stop. I'll admit all that talk of guns made me nervous, and I took more notice of the lone truck than I usually would. Our Wood's Ferry overnight was developing into a strange multidimensional outing. The campsite was an outpost of comfort on the trailing edge of our first day on the wild river, but the place was also easily accessible from Chester or Union, and therefore I felt a little anxiety about who might arrive next. We could not control who shared our evening with us, unlike our experience on Goat Island. If this land was the your land and our land and their land that Guthrie sang about, we couldn't keep them out.

Soon Venable went off in search of the Wood's Ferry hot shower we'd heard about. I found a dry spot where I could see both the truck and the river, and I took some notes. I watched the river in the rain. This time there was no Roger Lindsay in the parking lot. There was only that one lonely red pickup truck with a lockbox in the bed, the engine running, and the windows up.

In fifteen minutes Venable returned. He'd found the shower, and he crowed loudly about how it was indeed hot, even though it was open to the sky and the rain, and how he planned to take another shower before we left in the morning. Venable was happy and dry under the shelter, swabbing out his ears with a Q-tip. He looked out at the river and observed with a somber tone, "This is as close as I get to going to church."

As darkness descended, Venable took out the cook stove and sat it up on the picnic table. He heated water for tea. Foraging through my cook bag he noticed that I had brought along my ancient Sierra cup, the shallow metal camp cup made famous by John McPhee in *Encounters with the Archdruid*, a book about David Brower, director of the Sierra Club off and on for forty years. Venable picked up my cup and looked it over with disdain. I could tell by the angle of his eyebrow that he did not share McPhee's respect for the cup, from which McPhee and Brower had shared a sip of glacial water high in the Cascades.

"Oh God, that damn cup. This cup's why I never joined the Sierra Club," Venable said, tossing my cup back in the bag. "It's a worthless piece of shit. It's too shallow, unbalanced, and the metal brim burns your lips. I'm a member of a dozen other conservation organizations — Wilderness Society, Nature Conservancy, and on and on—but I've never joined the Sierra Club. Those other organizations never designed a worthless cup that became a symbol of their club."

"But you do look a little like John Muir," I said.

"John Muir's not responsible for that cup. Maybe David Brower, but not John Muir."

"David Brower is one of my heroes," I said. "He fought for wilderness."

"If David Brower invented that cup he should have been fired two decades earlier."

We ate dinner under the shelter. That night we consumed one of Venable's world-famous noodle splurges—a quick-cook noodle meal in a bag supplemented with two cans of precooked chicken. I'd brought plastic bowls for each of us. I filled mine to the brim. My choice of the plastic bowls kept Venable from heaping more ridicule on my Sierra cup.

After he finished Venable walked to the edge of the shelter. A blue Jeep Cherokee had joined the red pickup in the parking lot. The Jeep pulled up nose to butt with the truck. Venable watched until the Cherokee fishtailed away, slinging gravel. "What the hell are those people doing?" he asked. "Getting the jump on their neighbors for catfish season?"

After dinner the heavy rain subsided. I cleaned the dishes since Venable had cooked the dinners, and we set up our tent just outside the shelter. We spread out our sleeping pads and bags inside the tent. Then we retreated back to the shelter for storytelling. I told Venable about the crazy Wood's Ferry redneck on the white horse, and he launched into one of his best Alaska wilderness stories: "My brother John and I had been moose hunting up a remote river. We'd had a bush pilot drop us far upstream," Venable began. "Once we'd shot our moose, we planned to butcher it, pack the meat in dry bags, and raft down fourteen miles of class III–IV white water and another forty miles of fast water to our take-out in the nearest town."

That particular autumn the river rose due to heavy rains, and so rafting out added another level of excitement, he explained. To complicate matters more, they had shot a bull moose with a trophy rack of antlers and they decided they wanted to bring it back to have the head mounted for their father. "Before we launched, we lashed the moose head to the back of the raft so we wouldn't have to read the white water through the massive antler plates," he said, spreading his fingers wide to indicate the size of the bone plates.

They'd completed this wilderness trip many times but always with a second raft and other hunters. This time they'd been alone in a single raft. And, Venable said, due to the higher water level, "The easy rapids were tricky, and the two or three truly difficult constrictions were epic." In a class IV rapid—the entrance to the single class V rapid on the river—they flipped the raft due to the excessive weight of the moose head in the rear of the boat and the high water. Both brothers managed to swim to shore safely, but the upside-down raft continued downstream, heading deeper into the raging gorge. "We still had fifty miles before the take-out, and things didn't look good."

I sat listening in the dark to Venable's story play out. I could have been transported a hundred years earlier into a wilderness campsite and Venable could have been with Teddy Roosevelt entertaining at an outing of his famous Boone and Crockett Club.

"We ran along the shore, chasing the raft downstream as best we could," Venable continued. "About half a mile after the flip, the dangling moose antlers caught on a submerged gravel bar in the middle of the river, bringing the raft to a halt. John was able to swim out to it, reach underneath, and untie a throw bag and toss the rope to me on shore." When Venable tied the raft off to a tree and pulled it in they used a complicated river trick—a Z-drag—to recover the still fully loaded and very heavy raft.

There was only one way they could get safely to town: They sawed off the antlers and committed the massive head to the river. The meat, still lashed to the raft in dry bags, they kept, of course. "Scared and chastened, we got back on the river, not knowing if the rapids in the canyon would be worse due to the high water or washed out and easier. Some of both, it turned out," Venable said, finishing the story. "But we got to town, just at dark, happy, relieved, with the meat!"

Jimmy Buffett said once in a song, "And if you ever wonder why you ride the carousel / You do it for the stories you can tell." Our stories continued into the night, a songfest, a way of assuring clear passage through the Wood's Ferry thunderstorms, the unsettling locals, and the everyday sloughs of life. When we ran low of stories of our own, we made up ones about the locals driving through in their pickups.

The bad storms the fisherman at Lockhart had predicted arrived about nine. We heard thunder and watched lightning strike all around the campground. The rain fell in torrents for an hour. After the storm passed, I felt as if we might have a clear night. We crawled in our bags to sleep. I could hear the sounds of a South Carolina spring emerging. The chorus frogs sounded like sleigh bells in the flooded woods upstream.

⌒ Riding the Flood

On the morning of the fourth day, I stood by the river and watched debris come downstream from the upcountry—tree trunks, waterlogged lumber, oil drums, plastic bags, single shoes, beer coolers, and even a few basketballs. The river had risen two feet overnight, but the day dawned partly cloudy and breezy. Looking out across the muddy flow, I saw a chocolate-brown monster. The high water brought back the morning in Costa Rica three months earlier when Jeremy died. I felt a little fear. Venable walked up behind me and checked out the rising river. He sensed my apprehension and reassured me, saying, "There's nothing dangerous this morning on this big river once we get past that dam at Neal Shoals."

I'd been worried about high water since we got on the river. We'd seen so little rain in the piedmont the past few years that I didn't know how I'd react. We'd been in a severe drought in the upcountry, with no real sign—until that flood—of coming out of it. The Broad River / Santee River watershed historically had been subject to deep and persistent drought. The droughts in the nineteenth century had helped do in the canal system on the state's rivers, and big destructive floods in the early twentieth century had come close to bankrupting the fledgling Duke hydropower company. I reminded myself as I looked at the

Broad surging past that there was no such thing as a "normal" water level in a natural river system.

I recalled an oral history done nearby in 1937 by the Federal Writers' Project that I had discovered on the Internet before departure. Its subject was an African American named Richard Jones, who had been a slave on a Union County plantation owned by Richard Gist. Jones had been a boatman for twenty-four years on the Broad, taking Gist's cotton down the river from nearby Lockhart to Columbia. He worked the river in all its moods, and his oral account was rich in detail.

The boats Jones used to ply the Broad back then were known as bateaus, long, shallow-draft, flat-bottomed cargo craft pointed at the two ends. Bateaus, often built out of local planks, had been created by the French and replaced native dugout canoes. They were used on rivers all across North America. Because of their length (they could be up to sixty feet long) they were particularly good for carrying cotton downstream on South Carolina rivers.

Almost one hundred years old when he was interviewed, Jones recalled that every boat had a steersman, who would operate the long steering oar attached to the stern. There also was a headsman, who stood in the bow and helped the steersman navigate the rocky shoals. The less-experienced boatmen were known as privates. Jones described how Gist often sent three boats to Columbia, operated by as many as five slaves each. On these trips, they took meat, bread, and cabbage to eat and caught all the fish they wanted.

"They did the shoving and the heavy work," Jones told the interviewer. The privates also used paddles when it was necessary to add more power and stability to the craft.

During most of Jones's time on the river, he served in the more skilled post of steersman. The position of a bateau steersman on the Broad River was one of prestige in the limited world of a Union County slave. A steersman was a great deal like a riverboat pilot, someone who knew the river and understood how best to navigate in all conditions to get "Marse Gist's" cotton to market.

Jones said that sometimes when the Broad River rose the waves got as high as his cabin. When water was "a-roaring and a-foaming" all around them "like a mad tiger a-blowing his breath," Jones said he was always afraid he would lose his master's cotton. Sometimes the bateau would spin like a top, and the men would get so "swimmy-headed that you have to puke up all the victuals that you done eat." It took persistence and knowledge to get downstream: "You had to be up and doing something real fast."

Being a boatman was dangerous work, and the river wasn't the only danger. Jones described one steersman killed during a flood just downstream from Neal Shoals at a place called Fish Dam Ford. In high water a private accidently hit the man in the head with a paddle and knocked him overboard. They'd recovered his body and found no water in his lungs, so they were convinced the blow to the head had killed him.

"Us had de excitement on dem trips," Jones recounted for the WPA interviewer. "Lots of times water was deeper than a tree is high. Sometimes I was throwed and fell in de water. I rise up every time though." Maybe Richard Jones could become my spiritual guide as I continued my river trip. He'd survived many floods on the Broad, some so severe that he rode right over these very shoals on his bateau full of cotton "without a tremor."

Midmorning we broke camp, stowed all our dry gear in our watertight dry bags, loaded the canoe, and launched out on the surging Broad River. The current was strong for two miles to Neal Shoals Dam. We hardly paddled. Venable's steering strokes kept us straight, and the fast-moving water did the rest.

As soon as we identified the horizon line of Neal Shoals Dam ahead of us we stopped paddling. "It's strange to enter the backwaters behind a dam and yet to have such strong current," Venable said as we headed for the left shore.

We beached the canoe on the bank where a white sign nailed to a sycamore announced the upper end of the Neal Shoals portage trail. We stepped out of the canoe and walked down to the dam. There I saw why we'd made such good time: Neal Shoals Dam was a twenty-foot waterfall with two feet of floodwater surging over the top. I looked upstream from where we'd come. The whole surface of the narrow reservoir was a fast-moving river. "When we were here on our tune-up trip three years ago the river was low. We paddled right up to the lip of the dam and hopped over onto the dry bedrock below," I said, pointing to where we'd portaged. All we could see was dark water rushing over the brink.

Venable considered the power company's route around the dam and said he was insulted that they had roped off the take-out for the designated portage so far upstream. When we returned to the canoe, we launched and paddled further down the shore. I picked up the line of warning buoys and we slipped underneath. We worked slowly down the left shore. The sound of the pounding water going over the dam got louder as we approached it. I felt tippy in the canoe, though we were still a good fifty yards from the precipice when we took out. My heart was pumping when I finally stepped ashore. My arms felt light and I was giddy. But Venable was right: We were not in any real danger, and it made the portage much shorter.

All morning while we'd been on the river, despite Venable's assurances, a feeling of dread had been bothering me. It was more than just the high, fast, muddy water and its potential for danger, but that was definitely part of it. This was a something I'd never felt paddling white water in my twenties, thirties, or even forties. The feeling had been a constant companion for several miles. Maybe it was the ghost of Richard Jones haunting the river in flood times. Maybe it was simply a concession my brain had made to my body. I was aging, and I had not spent as much time on rivers lately as I had in my youth. My strength and skills had diminished, and bad things had happened on flooding rivers in the deep and near past.

I stepped ashore at Neal Shoals and quieted the dread. Standing above the dam I looked down at the pounding water and tried new names for what I was feeling. Maybe I could call it awe, or respect.

The portage path went up and over one end of the Neal Shoals Dam. We emptied the canoe, Venable took off with it, and I followed, ferrying the bags down the trail to quiet my nerves. At the dam we saw a fisherman who had stopped to check out the flooding river. On top of his pickup was tied a small johnboat, his standard gear for fishing the Broad at normal flows. As I passed he seemed puzzled, as if he thought, *What nut would be on the river in a canoe?* I walked by in silence with the last of our gear. He studied us as we loaded the canoe and ferried out among the flooded trees into the current. I guess he thought we knew something he didn't know about fishing the Broad. Maybe they were biting downstream.

As I carried gear on multiple trips from take-out to put-in I noticed an irritation where my river shoes were rubbing my heels. There was plenty of sand in my shoes and it began to rub me raw. I didn't think it was serious, but by the time we loaded the canoe I had to do my part barefoot. I had four large blisters on my heels and two where the top straps crossed my feet.

After we put back in below Neal Shoals the river was fast, but it was so wide we simply pointed downstream and rode the current. There were plenty of small shoals in this passage of the river, and we passed over them with no problems. On that day there were no rocks visible, no dangerous snags that I could see. At Fish Dam Ford, where Richard Jones had lost a companion, I'd expected to show Venable the remnant of an ancient fish dam—an ancient structure used for trapping fish— but it was buried under the heavy flow. There wasn't even a trace of it on the surface of the river. I had to fill Venable in on its history without a visual reference.

Remnants of ancient American Indian weirs, or fish dams, were not uncommon in southeastern rivers. Because they were constructed of rocks simply piled across the river, archaeologists can't easily calculate how old they are using their usual methods. The fish dam could have been in use continually for thousands of years. The zigzagging lines of boulders were placed in shallow river bottoms and formed a wide V with the mouth upstream. When the weirs were in use, a tapering cane basket was placed across the opening in the apex of the V. The current channeled fish into the basket, which made them easy to collect there at the dam. Back when the shad ran in the spring it would have been a busy place. The fish dam on the Broad River was listed on the National Register of Historic Places in 1973. At the time of the application the Fish Dam Ford trap was said to still be in very good condition "considering its long history," but there was no way to tell on this high-water day.

Downstream past the fish dam we stopped on the right bank and admired the muddy flow coming in from the Tyger River, which drains the western portion of Spartanburg County and the southern half of Union County. As we watched the discharge from the Tyger I could see sediment from Spartanburg and Union headed, like us, for the coast. A flood of mud had been washed into the stream from my hometown.

"More of the sloppy legacy of our Scots-Irish ancestors," I said as we watched the muddy flow from the Tyger merge with the Broad. "Up here in the piedmont the development business likes its regulations lax and their enforcement spotty. This stream is the color of a 'probusiness environment.'"

As we watched the Tyger River merge with the Broad, Venable vowed that someday we'd put in back in Spartanburg and paddle to the Broad on the Tyger, just for the heck of it. He collected rivers like he collected baseball cards as a kid.

The rest of the day we rode the surge like Richard Jones. I got comfortable enough to notice yellow jasmine and dogwood blooming in the woods, along with isolated redbuds. Coming past one of the islands that break up the expanse of the Broad River on the way to Columbia we spooked two deer and watched them swim back to the mainland. Not long after, a turkey flew over the river right in front of the canoe. "Hen," Venable said, watching as she reached the bank on the other side and ran into the brush. "She must have sailed a hundred and fifty yards." I took it as a good sign that the skies had cleared and the direction of the wind was in our favor. On a lark we even considered getting out the tarp, tying it to two spare paddles, and sailing downstream. In the end we decided it was too much trouble.

By late afternoon we made our goal for the night, Henderson Island, in the middle of Sumter National Forest. Henderson Island was the biggest of all the islands on the Broad, a mile long, all pine and hickory, with sandy alluvial soils. We set up our tent about halfway down the island on the western side. That night it was cold with lows in the forties as the windy front pushed on through. We stayed up after nine p.m., late on a river trip. I doctored my feet, put on dry socks and my pull-on Crocs. We talked little that night, merely watching the river and listening to night sounds. After a while Venable crawled in the tent to work on a crossword puzzle. Finding my first cell service since I left Spartanburg, I called Betsy.

I missed home, and I could hear in Betsy's voice that she missed having me there. She was worried about the weather. "Is the river flooded?" she asked.

"There's nothing to worry about," I assured her, adopting Venable's tone toward me from earlier in the day. "We're just riding the flood. We'll arrive in Columbia a little early is all."

By water Betsy was almost a hundred miles away, but by phone I could be fooled into believing she was right by my side. We had been through a great deal in the past two years—the close call Rob and Russell and I experienced on that December paddle on Lawson's Fork, the death of her mother, and the deaths of the two members of our party on that river in Costa Rica. But there was nothing but excitement in her voice as we talked that March night.

"Don't worry," I said.

"I know you're fine with Venable and soon you'll meet up with Steve," she said.

We slept that night close enough to the river to hear it surging past. The maps had shown a shoals at the head of the island, but the rocks were covered by the flood and no music of water over stone accompanied our rest. I woke up once and crawled outside. The sky was full of stars, and I was glad to see them.

ᑌᖇ Parr Shoals Reservoir

In 1969 the Wofford College River Voyageurs paddled across placid Parr Shoals Reservoir for what seemed, they wrote in their journal, "an eternity." Rather than eternity it sounded a little more like Hades. They described "paddling through an underwater forest of stumps," reporting that one canoe even hit a stump and nearly capsized.

Because of the high water level on our trip, Venable and I had an easier time of it on our fifth morning. There was little wind, and we set a relaxed pace in the slow backwater. Where a set of high-tension lines crossed the reservoir hundreds of cormorants roosted on the steel superstructure of the towers. We watched the birds as they sailed off the higher crosspieces and glided out across the lake. They looked prehistoric—like black, long-necked lizards—as they left their roosts. We paddled right underneath them and could hear the birds above making a strange keening sound. As we left the transmission towers and the cormorants behind I started looking for the cooling towers of the Virgil C. Summer Nuclear Generating Station, which would be our next major landmark. The Monticello Reservoir, a shallow cooling reservoir for the Summer nuclear station, mirrors Broad River's Parr Shoals Reservoir on the Fairfield County side of the river. The Summer plant came online in the antinuclear 1980s. "We'll soon see the ominous cooling towers of the plant as we paddle down the reservoir," I told Venable. "They always remind me of Jonathan Schell's *The Fate of the Earth* when I see them."

In 1982 when Schell's antinuclear apocalyptic narrative appeared, I was a highly impressionable twenty-eight year old. First I read the long series of articles in the *New Yorker*. Then I bought and read the book. I did not want the earth to become Schell's "republic of insects and grass." Nuclear holocaust, as a result of either someone pushing the red button or an accident at a nuclear plant, was the global warming of my generation. I bought a "No Nukes" T-shirt and the concert album to hear Carly Simon and James Taylor sing "Mockingbird." So did five hundred thousand other people under thirty.

In 1958, Pacific Gas and Electric planned to build the first commercial nuclear power plant in America in Bodega Bay, north of San Francisco, close to the San Andreas Fault. Local citizens began to protest the proposal soon after it was announced, and by 1964 the Sierra Club had helped to force the utility to abandon its plans for the plant. It was bad timing on the part of the nuclear energy movement. Its growth corresponded with that of the environmental movement in the United States. Public support for nuclear energy was strong in the late 1950s, but by the late 1960s it had diminished considerably.

By the mid-1970s antinuclear activism had moved beyond small local protests into a wider movement with growing influence. Though nuclear weapons were still a threat, the national movement focused on opposition to nuclear power. In the late seventies thousands were arrested nationwide at protests.

In March 1979 a partial core meltdown at Three Mile Island energized the movement even further. Though no one died at Three Mile Island, the accident was followed by the almost total shutdown of new nuclear plant construction in the United States. The release of the popular movie *The China Syndrome*, about a nuclear accident, twelve days before the Three Mile Island accident didn't help. It assured that there would be a public relations disaster for nuclear power.

That year hundreds of thousands of people turned out to protest nuclear power. In September almost two hundred thousand attended an anti–nuclear power rally in New York City. That same week in Madison Square Garden famous musicians put on their "No Nukes" concerts and released the popular album.

The nuclear climate in South Carolina was hot in 1979, as it was everywhere. There was reason for concern. South Carolina had the greatest concentration of nuclear facilities in the nation. Richard Riley, then the Democratic governor, wanted to slow the state's commitment to nuclear power. "We're loaded to the brim," Marion Brown, Riley's press secretary, told a reporter for the *New York Times* after the Three Mile Island meltdown. "If you measure downwind from one of the state's generating plants, you start getting fish with feet."

When Steve Patton reached Parr Shoals in 1981 he had to patch his canoe after a battering he'd received upstream in the numerous shoals. In his journal Steve said, "Don't feel so bad about using fiber glass and resin when I see a sign saying: NUCLEAR PLANT EXCLU-SION AREA. I feel bad about being here. At least the river is taking me away from here."

David Taylor doesn't even mention the nuclear plant in "The Ned Beatty and Me," detailing his trip through in 1999. By the time he gets to Parr he's still lost in his *Deliverance* reverie. He camped on the upper reaches of the lake and by the time he'd drifted off to sleep "whatever [Ned] Beatty fears I had had on the first two nights seemed now distant. I had felt the wildness of the rivers. That was enough."

Once the dam was in sight I had to admit to Venable that the nuclear plant hadn't exactly loomed above us as I'd remembered. We hadn't even seen the cooling towers, though my failed memory told me it had been a constant visage on the horizon on my earlier tune-up trip. Maybe what I was remembering was not the plant itself but the place that nuclear plants held for years in the imagination of all those of my generation.

South Carolina Electric and Gas, the operators of the Summer Station, have permits under review to expand their operation now that so many want to reopen the nuclear frontier. The current plant is licensed until 2042, so fretting about the plant may be useless, but as we paddled down the lake I told Venable I still believed our choice as a nation to shut down the expansion of nuclear power was a good one. "If my admiration for John McPhee has taught me anything, it's that all the best-laid engineering plans of human beings are likely to go bad given enough time." That, for me, was the subtext of both McPhee's *Encounters with the Archdruid* and *The Control of Nature*. "Sooner or later, nature will prevail, whether it's holding back the Mississippi or containing radiation in a deep hole."

As we paddled toward the dam, I talked more about the issue that concerns me most: nuclear waste disposal. I recounted for Venable the idea of the impossibility of communicating to those in the distant future the danger associated with nuclear waste, even waste buried deep in the earth in places like Yucca Mountain, Nevada.

"We can't communicate the danger for ten thousand years," I said. "Science fiction stories have taken on this problem. Language loses its meaning. Pictures lose their meaning." I explained how in 1981 linguist Thomas Sebeok was hired by the government to come up with a solution to this communication problem. He suggested the establishment of an "atomic priesthood" to pass the secrets along for millennia, but even that's probably impossible to execute.

Venable pointed out that by talking about elite priesthoods I was feeding the deepest fantasies that conservatives hold about environmentalists. "It suggests that you are willing to turn over the most important human needs to a select group of technicians. That doesn't sound like something a Romantic poet would profess."

"Do I contradict myself," I said, quoting Walt Whitman. "Very well, I contradict myself. I contain multitudes."

After another hour of paddling, the Parr Shoals Reservoir dam was finally in sight. At the dam there was no sign to point our way, no portage path like at Lockhart or Neal Shoals. The SCE&G people didn't seem to care whether a canoe got around their dam or not. First we paddled to one side to read a big red-and-white sign with floodlights under it that warned boaters "Spillway Ahead." Then we paddled back across the lake and down the southern shore until we saw a little cove with a vacation home up on stilts a few hundred yards upstream from the dam. Two black women, one old and one younger, sat fishing on an old dock. "Y'all catch anything?" they asked in unison when we floated up.

We introduced ourselves, said we'd come down from Spartanburg, and explained we weren't fishing. I said, "We're looking for a portage route around the dam."

"Spartanburg?" the older woman said incredulously. "How'd you get down here from Spartanburg?"

"The river," I explained. "The Broad River."

She looked confused and called out to a gentleman who'd walked out of the stilted house to see what was going on down at the dock. "Ricky, you know how they can get around that dam?"

Ricky seemed even less certain what we were asking than the women.

"Ain't no getting around that dam. You might as well go back where you come from. The power company don't want nobody around that dam. We can't even fish up there."

Undaunted, we said goodbye to the fishing party and paddled down to the dam anyway. I pointed out to Venable where I had portaged in

2006. "We simply ignored the safety barrier, paddled up to the end of the dam on river right, and hopped out on the grass bank," I said.

"Let's go back across the lake one more time and make sure there isn't a portage route on the other side at the power station," Venable said with an edge to his voice. "We'll do our due diligence."

So we paddled across the lake once more. With every stroke Venable was more and more vocal. "Can you believe the arrogance? Not a single sign of any sort about portaging."

I agreed. The lack of a sign put paddlers in danger as they probed closer to the dam looking for a short and usable portage.

We ferried about a hundred yards upstream in front of the dam, and the river was high enough so that there was a strong current pulling us toward the brink. We paddled hard and held our angle to the shore. I knew there was little chance we would flip, but the familiar knot in my stomach returned as we ferried from shore to shore. About halfway across we ran aground on a mud bank with cattails growing in it. I realized then that the lake was silted in and only five or six feet deep in front of the dam. If I fell out I could probably stand up on the muddy fill. Once we made the other side we checked out one more sign, but it didn't tell us anything new, so we paddled back across the lake to the place I'd portaged three years earlier.

The Parr dam "portage trail" was a beaten-down fishermen's path through an old trash dump and a stunted pine forest. We carried the first load of gear down as we scouted the best route. The grade was steep and the flooded river where we would put back in was fast and flowing through trees on what was usually shore. The portage took us three trips each, almost two hours.

Once all the gear was back at the river I looked upstream at the old Parr dam. Brown water roared over the top as it probably had a hundred times in flood events since it had been built in the 1930s. The water was headed for the low country where I was going. I might see it again in Lake Marion. From where we'd launch I couldn't see around the bend in the river, so I ran down the flooded shore until I could get a view of what was below. Downstream it looked like clear sailing. We relaunched in the flooded grove of sycamore trees, ferried out into the current, and headed downstream. By early evening we'd be on Haltiwanger Island, our last campsite before Columbia.

Between Parr Shoals and Haltiwanger Island we played a game of "Who can spot the eagle?" As we paddled we glanced down at the river channel to make sure it was clear, and then we shifted our attention quickly to the tall trees lining the shore. If one of us spotted a huge black bird with a white head resting on a dead tree, we would call out the sighting to the other. "Eagle! Two o'clock," Venable would say. I would answer, "Another at seven-thirty." We saw seven eagles that day.

The eagle population had recovered dramatically in South Carolina since the late seventies when in 1979 a survey of the state reported only thirty-nine sightings. In 2006 there were over five hundred, and the birds were nesting widely. One winter day a few years ago, Steve Patton and I spotted an eagle as far inland as the Lawson's Fork confluence with the Pacolet River.

In South Carolina the eagles are smaller than their northern kin, with wingspans only a little over six feet. An adult South Carolina eagle can weight seven pounds, but eagles from the northern range weigh twice as much. In spite of this, the eagles we saw looked plenty big to me. We slowed down a stroke or two each time we spotted them sitting on snags against the sky or soaring high above us.

Venable was used to eagles. In Alaska it's said there's an average of one eagle for every mile of shoreline. But my canoe partner seemed pleased to see them in such abundance in South Carolina. The eagles were part of what made the trip worthwhile for him, the signs of this rewilding of the South.

Cormorants were with us all day as well. Once we saw four that looked as if they were walking on water. When we canoed closer we saw that each was standing on its own dark snag just barely above the flooding river.

⌒ Haltiwanger Island

Our long portage at the Parr Shoals Reservoir dam had slowed us down. By the time we landed on Haltiwanger Island it was early evening and we were racing to make camp in the remaining light. We unloaded the canoe and set up quickly on a little saddle of sandy soil mostly clear of saplings. The river was still high and made a whooshing sound as it rushed through the narrow channel between the island and mainland. As we pitched the tent I could see feeding squads of dark swallows out over the river, and I could hear pulsing calls of chorus frogs somewhere up a nearby slough.

Once we had settled in, our campsite visibly excited Venable. He walked to the other side of the island and back. "My dad would have loved all this," he said when he returned. Then he became quieter than usual. "John and I are all that are left now," he said about his brother.

He pulled out his cell phone to call John in Georgia. "We made it past Parr dam and we're camped on a great island above Columbia," he told him. I listened as they chatted for a few more minutes.

Until listening in it hadn't occurred to me that Venable had his losses too. He'd lost his sister, Terrell; his father; and most recently his mother, Martha, in 2008. Now his direct connection to his southern roots was an empty midcentury modern ranch house in the suburbs, his long-distance friendships, and his hunting trips with his brother twice a year.

When Venable sat back down he said, "You know, going down a river is like a longitudinal study. Most people cross rivers on bridges, and they don't even glance down."

"We're seeing the whole thing," I said. "We're seeing it all."

We heard a passing freight train on the Southern Railway tracks on the northeast bank.

"Out there people are going about their lives, and we hear their trains, their dogs, their cars, but they never really see the river like we do," Venable said. He stood up and walked to the edge of the current. "We're here in this river corridor, and it could be a thousand years ago. It's a different way of seeing. They might come to see the river as we do with a little fishing, but that's as close as they get."

When Venable sat back down he became less reflective and more speculative. We bounced around ideas about how Haltiwanger Island got its name. Venable knew from his time as a lawyer in Columbia that the Haltiwangers were still a prominent family, and so it was probably named because they owned it, now or at one time. We also discussed how the island was on the border of what's known as the Dutch Fork, that area of the South Carolina midlands between the Broad and Saluda rivers settled by Dutch-Germans with surnames like Shealy, Sease, Bouknight, Bowers, Rikard, Kinard, Koon, Corley, Wessinger, Wise, Dreher, Derrick, Dominic, Geiger, Epting, Frick, Summer, and Huffstetler—and Haltiwanger.

In the mid-1700s these settlers, many of them recipients of land grants from the king of England, pioneered the land between the rivers. The German settlers stayed close to home, and few outsiders joined them. It's said those who settled the Dutch Fork created their own subculture with very particular ways. Many still spoke German well into the nineteenth century. Those who learned English had a dialect all their own. Friends of mine who grew up in Columbia in the mid–twentieth century told me that the children of those between the rivers tolerated a mild form of social discrimination. The Columbia teenag ers, mostly of English or Scots-Irish stock, wouldn't date the Dutch Forkers, even though their families had moved to the city. The Dutch Fork survived mostly through the presence of Lutheran churches and family names like Haltiwanger.

Names of places open a window into South Carolina's deep history. One of the earliest touchstones for such insight is Robert Mills's 1825 *Atlas of the State of South Carolina*, the first of an American state. A year later Mills published *Statistics of South Carolina*. Robert Mills took four years to complete the *Atlas* and the accompanying *Statistics*. There were twenty-eight district maps in Mills's *Atlas* when it was published. They were drawn from surveys taken over thousands of square miles.

Though Mills compiled the two works, they included the labor of at least two dozen surveyors, who covered every district in the state. The final district maps for which Mills made additions and corrections depicted waterways, towns, villages, roads, paths, good and bad land, rapids, waterfalls, and significant geographical features. The number of Mills's *Atlas* printed for the first edition is unknown, though a few survive in state libraries.

I encountered Mills's *Atlas* when I bought the most common reprint, the oversized 1980 edition with stamped fake gold leaf on its faux brown leather cover. When I decided to paddle to the sea I folded out the district maps from Abbeville to York one by one and poured over them. After I'd located the rivers that would be part of my journey I returned to those maps and traced my route through a nineteenth-century landscape. In my preparation Mills became a guide and a portal through which I could read the changes in the South Carolina landscape over nearly two hundred years.

Spend enough time scouring the maps in Mills's *Atlas* and you realize that the idea of wilderness is a modern conceit. Mills's early maps of South Carolina showed how familiar the territory had already become by the 1820s. On our trip we'd already passed a number of spots noted on Mills's maps: Trough Shoals, Grindal Shoals, Pinckneyville, Pinckneyville Ferry, Lockhart Shoals, the "Indian Mound," and Fish Dam Ford. Henderson's Island had already been named, but Haltiwanger was then known as Reeve's Island.

There were well-traveled roads running parallel to the river, and they crossed the waterway at key points by way of fords. There were even a few bridges on the smaller streams. A river trip that I was imagining as a journey, an adventure, had been, only two hundred years earlier, as common as a road trip on a present-day interstate highway.

In spite of hundreds of years of the human stamp of history and the present-day proximity to trains, Haltiwanger Island's most impressive feature was still its natural history. Much smaller than Henderson Island, Haltiwanger was rich in biodiversity. The island was thick with uncommon native plants that any naturalist would enjoy identifying. From where I sat waiting for dinner I could see holly, yucca, ironwood, jasmine, eastern red cedar, loblolly, and ten more plants I couldn't name. Behind me in the woods was a big stand of the early spring wildflower I knew as mayapple, just emerging and vibrant green.

Across the river in the dwindling light I saw Spanish moss hanging in the trees over the river. I was a little surprised. The plant was mostly associated with the slow, flat coastal plain, not the fast, rocky piedmont rivers like the Broad. Not a moss at all, Spanish moss is actually a bromeliad, a cousin to the pineapple. Known as one of the "air plants," it grows high in trees without roots and derives its nutrients from the wind and the rain. Looking a little like a gray beard, the plant summons up a sense of spooky southern weirdness.

There's probably no plant more associated with what's become known as Southern Gothic imagery in literature and culture than Spanish moss. Once used for insulation and mattress stuffing, it's now used mostly for arts and crafts, or to give that *Gone with the Wind* look to suburban yards.

Seeing Spanish moss hanging over small rocky shoals created a collision in my imagination. Its surprising location suggested to me that my expectations about sharp geographic boundaries were a little simpleminded. What was the piedmont really but a cascading series of fluctuating zones? In the piedmont, red hills and cotton were at the heart of our regional symbolism, not Spanish moss. In the piedmont we'd kept the cloying symbols of the Deep South at bay. Yet as we approached Columbia the natural symbolism had pressed in around me.

After a dinner of noodles and canned chicken we sat and listened to the river. I began to make out what I surmised was the distant traffic from Interstate 26. After that discovery it was hard to maintain any fantasies about the nineteenth century. Our talk turned to the approaching layover in Columbia. The flood had altered our plans. The original strategy had called for us to portage the Broad River Diversion Canal Dam on the outskirts of Columbia, work our way through the extensive fall-line shoals where the Broad River joins with the Saluda, and then end quite a long day at the Gervais Street take-out in the heart of the city, where John and Margie Zubizarreta, old friends of ours, would pick us up and haul us to their home.

Instead we decided we would take out at the Columbia Rowing Club a mile upstream from the diversion dam. That way we could have John and Margie drop us off at Gervais Street the next morning, bypassing the high water in fall-line shoals through Columbia, which we thought might be unnecessarily dangerous in our loaded canoe. Once we made the decision to portage around Columbia, we made a phone call to the Zubizarretas from Haltiwanger Island. We told them we were just four hours of paddling from our shower call at their house.

The Zubies were old river rats like us. I knew them when I worked at the Nantahala Outdoor Center twenty years earlier. Their history with Venable went back to the midseventies; they'd driven to Alaska to see him three times in the mideighties. Now a full professor at Columbia College, John spent most of his time surfing the academic rivers of English departments and professional organizations. Margie stayed at home with their two girls. They lived in the suburbs, in the very neighborhood Margie had grown up in, and mostly they paddled on the lake right across the street.

"We're riding the flood into Columbia tomorrow," I said to Margie.

"I've located our canoe racks in the garage. I'll put them on the minivan and pick you all up," she answered.

⌐ *Approaching the Fall Line*

The sixth day dawned clear and chilly. The water level had dropped two feet and the river had lost that deep mocha color of two days earlier. As Venable and I tied our gear in the canoe we talked about what has been neglected as people live their lives in modernity. Venable pulled the knot tight on the rope and said, "The modern digital generation might think nothing of value has been lost. Absolutely nothing. But think how many people have never heard a turkey gobble. That's what they're missing. Is it really important? I don't know how you can live an authentic life if you don't know what's going on in the natural world—how rainfall affects your rivers, your crops." He tied the cooler on top of the pile and we stepped in the canoe a final time before we reached Columbia. "Most people today just don't get it," Venable said as we shoved off from shore.

As we floated downstream I watched the wild shore passing. We were less than twenty miles from one of the South's old capital cities, yet on both sides was forest. The river was broken into braided channels. Hardwoods bent low overhead and each one had leafed out. There was no doubt about spring.

We were also approaching one of the East Coast's important geographic features—a northeast-southwest midstate zone known as the fall line. Strangely, the fall line is not really a line. It's where the hard crystalline rocks of the piedmont abut the softer sedimentary rocks of the coastal plain. It's an area defined by rocky outcrops and long stretches of rapids on all the major rivers and streams that cross it. Sometimes these rapids extend more than a mile. They defined river travel for centuries. The capitals of some of the states of the old Confederacy are located along this line—Richmond, Raleigh, Columbia, Atlanta, and Birmingham. "On each Atlantic-bound stream," Michael Godfrey explains in his *Field Guide to the Piedmont*, "rapids, and, in some cases, falls abruptly halted all but the most adventurous travelers."

On the river we were sheltered from the nearby modern world by an actual green, watery wildness. These linear river corridors could be one of the last remnants of wildness we have in the South—if not wilderness—that you can count on. On a cool April morning in 2009 it was possible to believe that this river corridor was our hope for contact with the actual world. Paddling was a way to leave some of the human chaos behind.

We began to see permanent houses along the shore. Each had an individual boat ramp to the river and a bank armored against the current with riprap or concrete. Every now and then a dock stuck out like a thumb into the current. There might be a right way to build a boat ramp on a river, but I never saw one on our trip to Columbia. They were mostly cheap, quick, and ugly. What's more, the riverine aesthetics of the homebuilders always tended in the opposite direction from my own. Most of the people who live on rivers in South Carolina know that it is their right as landowners to clear all the way to the waterline. Most either have not heard of riparian buffers (a strip of vegetation near a stream to help protect it from run-off) or exalt river views or access over conservation. River buffers have proven benefits. They slow water run-off, trap sediment, and enhance filtration. They capture fertilizers, pesticides, pathogens, and heavy metals, and they cut down on erosion. As we floated past more and more houses with chemically fertilized yards cleared all the way to the river, I wondered at what point regulation would reach our upstate rivers. We needed it.

The rest of the morning, we rode the high water toward the fall line. We wove in and out of islands, some large, some smaller than our canoe, and picked our way through shoals emerging as the water receded. Venable called out strokes, and we descended through broken ledges.

In 1969 Doc Stober's River Voyageurs had found this stretch of the river challenging. The morning of January 12, their fourth on the river, had dawned foggy, and they could hear the rapids below. They said the Lord's Prayer before setting off. Perhaps they should have said it twice. Just after they put in, Doc Stober and his paddling partner "approached the passage straight on and as they entered the gap between the rocks and trees, the inward current pushed the canoe closer and closer to the right bank." Doc was tangled in the low-hanging branches, and the canoe slipped under a submerged log and swamped in the current, continuing on down the rapids without Doc. The bowman stayed seated in the half-submerged canoe until it stopped on a rock. That January morning they built a fire to dry out paddlers and gear before continuing downstream to Columbia.

At one particularly large, river wide shoals a few miles above Columbia, Venable and I too watched cautiously from upstream as what we thought was a fisherman standing in a bass boat disappeared below the horizon line and reappeared a few seconds later. We were impressed with his bravery and willingness to risk a spill to keep on fishing.

We followed the fisherman's exact route to avoid a line of big curlers and a nice little ledge hole on our right. The route offered a good ride. When we gained on the fisherman we realized this bass boat was a particularly big log, and the fisherman we'd watched ride through the shoals was the root-ball with one long root forming the brave fisherman's profile in midcast.

Midday we finally passed under the I-20 bridge. Venable looked at his watch—almost noon. The energy of the fall line had helped us out. "We made about six miles per hour all morning. We were smoking."

I looked up and saw a Target truck roaring past northbound. All that time on the river and I had to be brought back to modern consciousness by a Target truck. "Expect More Pay Less," the side of the truck read.

"What's that supposed to mean? Does it mean that I will expect more than I actually get, or simply pay less no matter what I get?" The truck sped across the bridge at sixty or seventy miles per hour and was gone in mere seconds.

"It simply means we're back in civilization, Huck," Venable said.

It didn't take long to reenter the urban shadow. The skyscrapers of Columbia were less than a mile downstream, and this leg of the journey would be by minivan. Upon arrival at the rowing club dock, we saw two teenagers standing just downstream. They formed an unexpected welcoming committee I could have done without. One came running up when we landed. He was dressed in low-rider jeans, basketball high-tops with the strings loose, and a flat-brimmed ball cap turned at a forty-five-degree angle to his face. It was the middle of the day on a Tuesday, so he must have been skipping school. He smiled and announced, "Hey, we got a big snake down there. I think we're gonna kill it."

"Don't kill it," I said, the outrage triggered. "It's probably just a harmless water snake."

"No, I think we'll kill it," he said and ran back down the trail to join his partner in herpetological crime. I was fuming as we unloaded the boat. I kept glancing down the trail toward where the two young men were hurling large stones at the helpless snake. As much as anything—the useless dams, the streambank destruction, the sediment clouding the river, the garbage along the shore and strewn in the trees—this incident with the water snake expressed the disconnect of the modern world with the natural world.

"What's a snake good for?" a friend had asked me once after a copperhead had bitten her family's big friendly Weimaraner on the face and front leg. The dog swelled up as big as Porky Pig but survived. "I'd get rid of them all," she said. "Every last one of them."

I know there's danger—the rare bite of a poisonous snake—but that's not enough for me to want to vote snakes off the planet. We've already eliminated cougars, black bears, elk, the Carolina parakeet, the woodland buffalo. I imagine all the habitat turned to subdivision since we arrived in the eighteenth century with our primary set of human needs, all the game trails paved and leading somewhere important to us—cities, towns, malls.

In spite of it all, snakes are still among us. They're survivors, a living link to wildness and deep time, though even the poets aren't always kind to them. Mary Oliver describes a water snake preferring "sweet black water and weeds" to her company, and James Dickey warned of snakes lurking in the kudzu, "striking under the leaf heads." In spite of what other poets say, I count snakes among the creatures I most admire.

By the time we had everything out of the canoe, the teenagers brought the snake over to show us. They held it out on a stick like children with a prize they'd won. I was right. They'd killed a nonpoisonous banded water snake. The snake's head was unrecognizable after repeated assault. I turned away disgusted, grabbed the dry bags, and began hauling them up the gravel trail to where Margie would meet us.

⤳ Columbia Layover

The arrival in Columbia marked a transition in the trip, as it had for some of the travelers I'd studied before departure. In 1880 Spartanburg's Garner brothers spent two or three days in Columbia on their paddle to the sea. Upstream, the waters of the Broad River had been familiar territory to them. They'd made several trips to Columbia in cotton boats. They rested in the capital city before continuing down the Congaree, which was *agua incognito* for them.

The Wofford River Voyageurs arrived in Columbia about two p.m. on January 12, 1969, with much fanfare. *The State* newspaper and several television crews met them at the old diversion dam for the Columbia Canal, where they set up camp. They talked to the reporter that afternoon, but the story never ran. The New York Jets, who beat the Baltimore Colts in the Super Bowl that Sunday, must have bumped them, because the paper the next morning was full of stories about the game. One voyager's mother brought him a birthday cake, and Wofford biology professor Gibbes Patton drove down from Spartanburg to restock the expedition with canned goods. He also talked with team members about their botany projects.

Harold Shreiner, their tour planner in Columbia, took wet sleeping bags to a washateria and then ferried the group to the YMCA for showers and to a drugstore to buy candy. That night they ate chili. They were in bed by midnight.

The next day the River Voyageurs toured Columbia. They were supposed to meet with Governor McNair, but he was out that day with the flu. Instead they toured the state capitol and the new Carolina Coliseum. At noon they departed for lunch in the revolving restaurant on top of Capstone dormitory, but it was closed. They ate in another dining hall on campus amid a "host of pretty girls." However, their appearance was "not glamorous nor our manners very good . . . seventeen men who had been used to camping out just about went wild in the presence of a women's dorm."

That night they drove out of Columbia and camped at the Highway 76 bridge on the Wateree River. Doc Stober stopped and bought boxed chicken dinners for everyone. There they met with Henry Savage on his home river, the Wateree, and talked with the writer about his book.

In 1981 when Steve Patton arrived in Columbia, he met a friend at the diversion dam who showed him where to hide his canoe and took him to fill his water jug and buy supplies at the Piggly Wiggly. That night Steve talked to his friend half the night and crashed on his couch at an apartment near the river.

Next day at dawn Steve worked his way downstream through the dry riverbed of the last reaches of the Broad River. He had found the rocky river "a very good learning place for rank novices . . . only the foolhardy who like to repair things should try it in a wood and canvas canoe." All day he worked his way through the shoals along the Broad/ Saluda River fall line. "Damn Columbia. Damn the canal," he wrote. "If you make this trip for fun, definitely truck your canoe around Columbia."

David Taylor had not read Steve's journal when he made the trip in June 1999. Barefoot, tired, and frustrated, he'd arrived at the diversion canal dam on the morning of his fourth day on the river. He slipped over the rocks at one end of the dam, and a fisherman noticed he was barefoot. "Where's your shoes, man? Ain't you scared of snakes?" David laughed because the fisherman thought he "was some wild man from the streets."

After struggling through the same shoals that had defeated Steve twenty-eight years earlier, David pulled "the Ned Beatty" ashore at the foot of the Gervais Street Bridge. He had finally merged with the Saluda and was standing in the waters of the Congaree in Columbia. His journey was over. The first thing he did upon landing was to ask directions to the nearest bar. "The Bass ale I ordered was sweet, and the bartender suggested a chicken cordon bleu sandwich to buffer the switch from Ramen." At the end of his essay David reflected on what he'd learned: "A landscape that I had imagined as commonplace and dull, I now see as a wilderness. . . . The wilderness is there if we trust it is and choose to enter it."

I was a little relieved as well when midafternoon of our sixth day we left the linear river wilderness of the Broad River in Margie's minivan for what would be an evening of human respite—food, conversation, laughter, laundry, and showers. We lashed the canoe on the roof racks and stowed our gear in the hatchback. Margie drove us a few miles to Forest Acres, the 1960s subdivision on the east side of Columbia where she lived across the street from her childhood home with her husband, John, and their two daughters, Anna Ruth and Maria.

On the drive we filled Margie in on our adventures and recovered our sense of shore time. We noted how just downstream from where we took out we would have passed the fall line, the last rapids of the

Broad River, and the confluence of two great upstate rivers, the Broad and the Saluda.

The last fall-line rapids were not entirely foreign to me. One summer day in 2007 I'd driven to Columbia with Steve to scout the Broad and Congaree rivers at the fall line. The water was low that day, but I still wanted to check out that shallow, rocky passage of the Broad I'd always crossed by car on I-126 coming into the capital city.

Columbia was destined to become a city in 1786 when the South Carolina General Assembly decreed that the state government should move from Charleston to the midlands. At the confluence of major rivers, the fledgling town of Columbia was ideally situated for growing statewide commerce as the backcountry opened up.

At the dawn of the nineteenth century the only reliable way to move quantities of goods was by river, and so South Carolina embarked on an expensive statewide canal system. Beginning in 1819, the state would sink a stunning percentage of its revenue into eight canals—four on the Catawba and Wateree Rivers, two on the Broad River, at Columbia and Lockhart (opening up 110 miles of the Broad River above Columbia), and two on the Saluda River. Once all the canals were constructed, the entire state, except Greenville, would be accessible by river. But as contemporary historian Walter Edgar explains in his *South Carolina: A History*, "Despite the twenty-five miles of canals and fifty-nine locks, poor routes were selected because of politics, and the public did not use the canals. As a result not enough revenue was collected to pay the lockkeepers' salaries. By 1838 six of the eight had been abandoned."

The state began the Columbia Canal on the Broad River in 1819 and completed it in 1824. The guard lock for the three-mile-long barge canal was situated at the top of today's diversion canal. The canal now provides electricity for South Carolina Electric and Gas. Today it produces about eleven megawatts of power and diverts up to six thousand cubic feet per second of water from the main channel of the Broad River.

In July 2006 a $5.5 million fish-passage facility, or fishway, opened at the diversion dam on the Broad River. The structure is a "vertical slot ladder" designed to allow the migration of fish upstream. The fish ladder is a set of low steps; the water's velocity has to be high enough to attract the fish to the ladder, but it cannot be so great that the fish will be washed back downstream or are exhausted to the point where they cannot complete their journey.

The Broad River Fish Passage was the first fish passage facility in South Carolina not under federal control, for such migrating fish as shad and sturgeon. The ladder provides access to two-dozen miles of the Broad River and tributaries that had been blocked since the early 1800s.

In July 2006, when Steve and I set out down the Broad River on our scouting trip, the water coming down the fish ladder was so low we could walk it. There were no fish to be seen climbing the ladder, but it was well after the spring migration season. The old saying goes that in the summer the only thing between Hades and Columbia is a screen door, but there are also several rivers flowing between. That summer there were a million Carolinians sweltering in the heat in all directions, and downstream from the diversion canal I admired two fishermen who had beached their aluminum canoe in the shallows and sat belly-deep in fold-out chairs, cooling off.

When Steve and I reached the confluence of the Broad with the Saluda River, the newly joined waters of the two rivers proved icy cold. College students in inner tubes bobbed past pulling sidecars with coolers. The river looked like a watery city park. The Saluda River is released off the bottom of the Lake Murray Dam, and so the midland current is cold enough for mountain trout. We took one more dip to cool down in the first few hundred yards of the Congaree River before getting out at the Gervais Street Bridge in the midday Columbia heat.

Spring was at full tilt by the time Venable and I arrived in John and Margie's Columbia suburb. Azaleas and dogwoods were at peak bloom in the yards we passed. The stoked-up banks of blooms formed mustaches along the front of every suburban house. They looked a little revolting. The scene was too much for me. White, pink, yellow, orange, and red flashed in from every direction. These domestic cultivars of the same native plants we'd passed on the river looked comically obscene, almost pornographic. As we drove slowly past the lakes and deeper into the pine-lined subdivision, I had a *Twin Peaks* moment. Nothing seemed real in the Columbia suburbs, and I was caught in a manufactured Technicolor dream of someone else's making.

When we pulled into the sandy drive of John and Margie's house, reality returned, and the dream receded. The Zubies live in an old brick house, and the front garage door was open, revealing their vintage paddles, life vests, spray jackets, and fishing gear, all stowed in every nook and cranny. I felt comforted and grounded by all my friends' gear, which assured me I was once again among my tribe.

John, whom we call Zubie, is Cuban American and grew up an immigrant city boy in New York City at the base of Triborough Bridge. When he was sixteen, he'd moved with his family to Miami and attended the university there. When Zubie left Miami in 1973 for the PhD program in English at the University of South Carolina, he'd driven up I-95, but the highway wasn't finished yet, and so soon after he'd crossed the Florida line he'd shifted from interstate to U.S. 301. He'd followed it all the way to Columbia. That road trip was an eye-opener for the immigrant boy. He'd never seen the typical southern landscape—cotton fields, shacks, and people sitting on porches. The scenes were just like the rural South his beloved Flannery O'Connor described in many stories.

Finally cresting a hill on U.S. 301 outside Columbia, Zubie had seen the city's only tall building in the distance and realized he'd made it. Graduate work in English soon grounded Zubie in southern literature, but he also developed a passion for white-water paddling. He learned to paddle tandem canoe and solo decked canoe (C-1) on Appalachian mountain rivers on weekend trips and worked guiding rafts several summers for the fledgling Nantahala Outdoor Center (NOC). Three years after driving up from Miami, Zubie founded the USC white-water club. At its organizational meeting he'd met Margie, his future wife, and Venable, another paddler who would become one of his oldest, best friends and best man at his wedding. The three of them had paddled together for many years.

Zubie, Margie, and Venable stayed in close contact when Venable left for Alaska in the early eighties. On their trips to visit him in Alaska Zubie and Margie had fished and explored rivers with Venable. A few years later Zubie had returned solo to Alaska to do a lengthy river trip with Venable north of the Brooks Range. They were old friends, comfortable with each other under any circumstances.

The Zubie house in Columbia was a perfect place for us to layover before continuing downstream. That afternoon I stayed behind at the house to wash clothes and catch up on note taking. Margie ran errands and attended one of the girls' soccer games. Zubie and Venable drove to a grocery store to buy fish for the grill and restock for the rest of our trip. When they returned, Zubie marinated the fish he'd bought in a basic Cuban recipe, a *mojo*, made of lime, olive oil, and lots of garlic.

Zubie is a smaller version of Venable, minus the beard and with a higher metabolism. I watched as he moved between the outside grill and the kitchen with the same energy used to attack his teaching of literature and his river running. Zubie may even be more verbal than Harvard grad Venable. When they were together, it was as if you'd combined some volatile linguistic compound and the resulting combustion was class V storytelling. As we ate our dinner of grilled fish and sweet potatoes several wild yarns unfolded, one in particular about a mutual friend who had also been at that first USC white-water club meeting— Hobie Buffington.

"Hobie was a legend in our circle of friends—good-looking, studly young kid—always a babe magnet," Zubie started, with a big smile on his face. "We'd worked together at NOC and then Hobie went to New Zealand to guide rafts. He'd returned with a wife, and Margie and I took the newly married couple out to Lake Murray. The visit got off to a bad start when the boogie board the young bride was riding in the wake hopped up and slapped her in the face and broke her nose."

But that was all lead-in to the best part of the story: "Hobie convinced his young bride to accompany him on a honeymoon float trip down the Congaree. It was low water. They came to one of those muddy Congaree beaches and Hobie looked over and saw a wild pig. He landed the canoe, got out his rifle, and shot the pig and threw the carcass in the canoe. That night Hobie butchered the pig on the beach and served it up to his new bride. Not long after that she went back to New Zealand, and I've always thought it was that pig that did them in."

"Didn't Hobie do a stint as a catfisherman on Lake Marion?" Venable asked, baiting the hook for a long-familiar story told and retold many times.

"I'd go down there and run Hobie's trotlines with him," Zubie continued. "We'd come back with a skiff full of catfish. He bought this depth finder and told me how the cats like to lounge off these fifteen-foot-deep ridges in the lake. 'We're at fifteen feet now,' Hobie said, looking at his newfangled depth finder. I stuck my paddle in the water and it was about three feet deep. Hobie ripped that gadget out and threw it in the lake."

I slept in a bed that night awash with river stories. I surfed their rocky current toward sleep, thinking about the survival of friendship over decades. I was lucky to have such longtime friends as Venable, Margie, and Zubie, and I thought about how rivers have tied us together all these years. Rivers are the central theme in our lives as they are in those of thousands of others, those people I've always called members of my paddling tribe. Zubie may never had met Margie or Venable had he not started the white-water club at USC, and I may never have met Venable had I not written a book about the Chattooga River.

I'd made it halfway down the river. I was primed for such meta-phoric musings, and so I lay awake thinking them through. What stands between us and some other watershed of experience? A choice here, a little luck there, the following of a passion we couldn't even see coming. Had Betsy and I ended up in that other raft in Costa Rica I might be hip deep in grief for the loss of a loved one, or I might have drowned like Jeremy. All that separates us from who we are and who we might have become is one or more turns in life. There was no answer, no conclusion, so sleep finally found me. If I dreamed that night in Columbia I made no note of it.

◡ Green Diamond

The morning of the seventh day, I showered once more for good measure. I helped Venable pack our clean and dry gear in the minivan, and
we ate pancakes Zubie had filled with leftover sweet potatoes from the
night before. Margie checked the Internet to see what weather was in
store for us. She said we could expect two more days of showers, so
there would be no respite from the rain. There were flood warnings
for both the Congaree and Santee rivers. Our gear was finally dry, but I
knew it would be wet again by nightfall.

After we finished the pancakes, we spread our topo maps on the
dining room table, the corners held down by coffee cups. This leg of
our journey would take us out of Columbia's central urban core, under I 77, and finally, by day's end, into some of the wildest country in
South Carolina—the Congaree National Park. The day would be long,
even with the river running high. Several weeks before, I'd called the
park and asked about camping in the river corridor. There's only one
backcountry campsite, and the ranger told me there was no reservation
system. "First come, first serve, but you should be fine on a Wednesday
night in early April." We would need to paddle about twenty-seven
miles from Columbia to get there.

Zubie had early responsibilities at Columbia College, so we said
goodbye in the driveway, and Margie drove us back to our downtown
Gervais Street launch site. Venable and Margie talked in the car about

their past river adventures in the Southeast and Alaska, and I could tell Margie missed rivers. She said she wished she could go with us. The night before I'd noticed how she'd asked questions about the river upstream as she looked at our topo maps with longing. After hearing our stories about the beauty of the passage between Parr Lake and Columbia, Margie said, "We might take the girls on an overnight soon up on the Broad River."

A little after nine a.m. we pulled up to the Gervais Street put-in at the foot of the elegant old Gervais Street Bridge. It was the earliest and most decorative of the three bridges now crossing the river. The site historically has served several bridges and early ferries. The ferry into Columbia from the west was first replaced in about 1791 by a toll bridge. A wooden bridge across the river was completed about 1827. The bridge was burned in 1865 before General W. T. Sherman's army entered the city.

The present bridge was built in 1928, and at the time it held the widest roadway in the state. From 1928 until 1953 the Gervais Street Bridge was the only bridge across the Congaree River. A recently built riverside park celebrates the river history with interpretive plaques and is a morning gathering spot for urban trail-walkers taking advantage of the extensive riverside trail along the Congaree. When we arrived, there were two elderly women at the Gervais Street boat launch just back from their morning walk. From their perch on a rock retaining wall they looked at the rising river, looked back at us, and asked with concern, "You're not canoeing on that are you?"

Venable smiled, said, "Yes ma'am, we are." The women shook their heads and watched as we walked our bags of gear down to the put-in as if they were watching the loading of a hearse.

The sky was overcast though it was not raining. The cottony clouds hung around the tops of the high office buildings in downtown Columbia. That didn't bode well for the day. We would be wet soon enough. Margie and I went back to the minivan and carried the remainder of the dry bags down. Once again, Venable shouldered the canoe and walked it down. We lashed in our gear, said goodbye to our host for a night in Columbia, and pushed off into the current.

As we cast off I looked up at the Gervais Street Bridge with its elegant arches and streetlights. The structure spoke of a classic age when crossing a river was an event. Bridges were built to be beautiful back then, designed with perfect proportions and lines. They were a part of the public works consciousness that sought to create structures that were both pleasing and practical. Now the bottom line determines the look of most bridges. Modern bridges are built of cast concrete and do little more than extend the roadway. Too often they block the view of the river and our ability to commune with it.

As I looked up at the bridge, I thought about where we had come from and where we were going. We'd paddled one set of the branching lines in the vast web of this giant river system. Above where we put in and above its confluence with the Pacolet, the Broad River stretches into North Carolina. To the south, one of the Pacolet's sister rivers, the Saluda, rises in the mountains above Greenville County and drowns under the waters of vast Lake Murray just before it reaches Columbia. To the north the Catawba/Wateree system drains half the North Carolina piedmont, including Charlotte. The Catawba rises in the Blue Ridge in western McDowell County about twenty miles east of Asheville, flows mostly east, then forms Lake James after its confluence with the Linville River; then it passes north of Morganton and through the Lake Norman reservoir. After it leaves Lake Norman, the river passes Charlotte, then through Mountain Island Lake and Lake Wylie, where it finally forms ten miles of the border between North

Carolina and South Carolina. Once the river enters South Carolina it passes Rock Hill and then through the reservoir at Great Falls.

The falls of the Catawba at Great Falls, South Carolina, remain pretty great. Historically the falls were four miles long, with a total drop of 121 feet. The creation of the dams to generate electricity at Great Falls dried up the top two miles of the vast shoals except during times of flood. Another reservoir on a smaller tributary drowns the bottom two miles. In 2006, interested groups looked into recovering the top two miles of the great falls for recreation by altering the dam and restoring flow to the dewatered stretch. They convinced Duke Power of the need for recreation and a 2007 relicensing agreement assured some releases for white water at Great Falls.

Downstream from Great Falls the Catawba flows into Lake Wateree. By the end of the Catawba's fall through the piedmont, almost the entirety of its head has been used by the power companies. The wild river that churned downstream through seasonal floods and droughts for millions of years now spreads out into many lakes where it is caught behind dams. What's lost when a river is drowned behind each dam and an artificial lake replaces a real river for those fishing or waterskiing?

During the writing of *River of the Carolinas* Henry Savage pondered the vastness of this river system we were descending. He knew that those on the lower Santee would not connect their slow, meandering river with the rocky tributaries like the Pacolet River and the Linville River in the South and North Carolina upcountry. In a 1955 letter to his editors Savage said that he wanted a name more inclusive than *River of the Carolinas* and suggested *The Santee System* to solve the problem. Savage was afraid "that many people that may be very interested in the Catawba or Saluda will not realize that *River of the Carolinas* is the story of their river." *The Santee System* was deemed too technical sounding, and the solution Savage and the editor came up with was to add "The Santee" to *River of the Carolinas* as a subtitle.

We were back on the river. The Congaree was three or four hundred feet wide there at our Columbia put-in point on the West Columbia side. I had only one more night with Venable on this first leg of my paddle to the sea. There was only one more major branch to add to the Santee System—the Catawba/Wateree's confluence in the swamps below the U.S. 601 bridge—and in a couple of days Henry Savage's whole Santee would be complete.

I felt there at Columbia something significant had changed about the river and our trip. From the fall line downstream, the Congaree had been a working-class river for well over two centuries, providing a transportation route. The Congaree waters below Columbia were more predictable and suited to commercial travel. In the nineteenth century steamboats had plied the river, and today it's navigable by motorboats all the way up from the coast. Ours would be a different experience now that we were about to embark on paddling the main stem of the Congaree/Santee.

In contrast, above the fall line the difficult, shoal-filled Broad, Saluda, and Catawba rivers had proved almost impossible to pull into service. The elaborate canal system Robert Mills had conceived, though intricately engineered, failed as a method of opening the upcountry to market commerce. The rivers, like the Scots-Irish who settled the upcountry, had proved stubborn and resistant to authority. When the railroads made their way to Spartanburg and Greenville in the 1850s, upcountry farmers finally had a reliable method of getting their goods to market.

The rain held off, but the Congaree was already high. A few miles below our urban Columbia launch site, the river meandered past a large floodplain on the left bank. A decade earlier a low-country real estate company called Burroughs and Chapin tried to develop 4,600 acres here for a sprawling office park, convention center, and residential community. The developer had made its reputation building Sunbelt resorts and retirement communities in Myrtle Beach, contributing to the South's coastal development boom of the 1990s. But as the decade drew to a close, Burroughs and Chapin had outgrown the coast and migrated inland, planning for Columbia and the Congaree the $1 billion development it called Green Diamond.

Although 70 percent of the Burroughs and Chapin property was on flood-prone bottomland restricted from development, the company lobbied FEMA (Federal Emergency Management Agency) to redraw the floodway lines of the Congaree, in effect, making the floodplain a legal place to build. FEMA's final decision on the Congaree map reverberated throughout the South. The agency ruled against Burroughs and Chapin, blocking the huge developer's plans for the Green Diamond.

Environmentalists throughout the South saw the fight over the Green Diamond as a kind of referendum on an increasingly complicated question facing the region: How much of the health, safety, and quality of life of our communities and ecosystems are we willing to sacrifice for economic growth?

For Burroughs and Chapin the answer seemed to be as much as they could legally get away with. Its supporters in Columbia lauded the economic growth Green Diamond would spur and saw the old levee on the Congaree, beefed up with modern engineering, as an adequate safeguard against flooding. Opponents cited the strength of recent hurricanes such as Hugo and Floyd as evidence that moving thousands of people into a floodplain could spell disaster. Then Katrina confirmed everybody's worst nightmares about worst-case-scenario flooding. It's hard to say "levee" any longer and not have someone file a lawsuit.

As we floated past the site, I told Venable, "This is one the most important battlefields in southeastern environmental history. The environmentalists' victory here will become even more important later."

Venable agreed the land along the Congaree offers a much-needed tract of green space below Columbia, but as a long-practicing attorney he inserted some skepticism: "The ruling by FEMA reaffirms the current floodplain lines but that doesn't guarantee the ruling will hold in the future. Burroughs and Chapin backed off their development, but that doesn't mean somebody else more powerful won't bring it up in the future." He had a good point. Developers never go away if they see a buck to be made.

As we floated below the Green Diamond we detected the odor of chlorine. "Columbia's sewer treatment plant," I said. The odor was distinct and burned my nose. We paddled over near where a bubbling, submerged pipe on the north bank of the river released effluent into the Congaree. "Sewage on one side," I said, "and on the Cayce side, a steel mill. We've got a little piece of Germany's industrial Ruhr Valley right here in South Carolina."

We were paddling between an environmental Scylla and Charybdis. Could we have been closer to an environmentalist's hell? But I knew from reading up on all the industry along the river that things were not that simple. In 2004 SMI Steel was honored for its recycling success, diverting materials from its waste stream. They may make rebar at SMI, but they recycled too.

We left the Green Diamond, the sewage plant, and the steel mill behind and slipped under the I-77 bridge, our last road crossing before U.S. 601 some fifty miles downstream. In an eerie coincidence I looked up at the interstate and saw yet another Target truck overhead—"Expect More Pay Less," a semi once again proclaimed from above. What were the chances of the same phrase punctuating both the entry and exit to the only major urban area on our trip? Why was it that a marketing koan was destined to follow me down the river? I started to try to connect the dots—target, more, less, expectations. As we passed underneath I-77 I looked back and counted and multiplied, looking to numbers for some understanding: A hundred trucks and cars passed in the minute I counted, so 6,000 vehicles would pass every hour. How many of them could possibly be Target trucks, and what could it possibly mean that I'd seen one pass overhead each time we paddled under an interstate highway? I knew I was digging pretty hard with my paddle for mystical connections in the sediment-laden waters of the Congaree. I laid it out for Venable and asked, "What does it all mean?"

Venable laughed and said, "It might not mean anything. If we did a little research we'd probably discover a huge Target distribution center nearby."

"It has to mean something," I said, but I realized right away that I was a little punch-drunk on river time. I'd started to feel a little of what David Taylor had experienced paddling by himself on the Broad River a decade earlier. I was like Huck Finn's companion, Jim. I was looking for portents, for signs, for meanings in everything I observed; the more time I spent on the river, the more it seemed to me alive, an animate living creature flowing to the sea. If the river was alive, then maybe it was connected outward to all the things passing over and around it, maybe even a lowly Target truck. There was meaning in the web of life (even the life of the interstate), and I was going to find it.

Paying attention to the passing riverbanks brought me back to a more contemporary reality. The signs of spring were now more than new leaves on individual trees. Both banks of the river were thick with recently emerged foliage. There were more willows and fewer of the trees that are plentiful in the piedmont—box elders, birches, and sycamores. The littoral nature was changing as we floated farther downstream.

Nature might have been changing, but human nature stayed constant below Columbia. We paddled past a hunt club on the east bank with huge white signs that announced, "No Trespassing—High Powered Rifles." It was enough to keep me from landing. Someone had once told me that downstream on the Congaree there was a massive legendary exclusive club where politicians and fat cats went to hunt and carouse when the state house wasn't in session. I wondered if that mythic hunt club was what was inland behind the imposing signs. Venable said that the story sounded like the makings of a hit musical about South Carolina's often-comic political scene but that he didn't know how we'd prove its truth for a nonfiction narrative. "But as has been said before," he concluded, "in a contest between truth and legend, always print the legend."

⌇ Congaree

We stopped for lunch on a rare Congaree River sandbar and ate summer sausage and crackers. Thirty years earlier when Venable was in law school at the University of South Carolina, he had paddled this very stretch of river on a difficult two-day solo trip when the river was much lower and speckled with sandbars. His father, Bunn, had paddled the Congaree in flood as a young man in the 1940s and often had told Venable the story of escaping the river before nightfall and spending the night in a local bootlegger's shack.

As we ate lunch, Venable and I talked about what awaited us downstream: the eleven thousand acres of old-growth floodplain protected in the holdings of the Congaree National Park. Surely with so much public land on the left bank we'd find a safe sheltered place to camp, even in high water. After lunch, back in our canoe, we passed miles of wide floodplain stippled with second- and third-growth trees. In 1800 there had been over a million acres of old-growth floodplain forests along the rivers in the low country of South Carolina. In the 1830s slave labor was used to construct dikes at the northwest and southwest boundaries of the swamp. Later there were efforts to graze cattle there, an attempt to make the "useless" land of the dried-out swamp productive. Logging continued in the Congaree Swamp into the nineteenth century. In the 1950s local conservationist Harry Hampton recognized the value of vanishing old-growth river swamps, and through his efforts and those of others, the vast floodplain was finally protected in 1976 as the Congaree Swamp National Monument. In 2003 the swamp became Congaree National Park, the first national park in South Carolina and one of less than a dozen in the Southeast. Today a large part of the museum in the park headquarters is dedicated to Hampton and the early conservationists.

The woods below Columbia, like the river, had always been worked hard. In the late nineteenth and early twentieth centuries the lumber industry pulled millions of board feet of cypress, tupelo, sweet gum, and a dozen other species out of these intact river swamps. Today there are only thirteen thousand wooded acres left. With the destruction of the swamps came the loss of valuable habitat for species such as black bears, cougars, river otters, and the iconic old-growth-dependent ivory-billed woodpeckers. In South Carolina the bears and otters had made a comeback, but in spite of extensive searches in the Congaree there was still no sign of surviving ivorybills.

Then on February 11, 2004, kayaker Gene Sparling caught a glimpse of a large and majestic woodpecker in the Cache River National Wildlife Refuge of Arkansas, and the sighting began a scientific search for a species that most believed extinct. Since then, there have been additional sightings and a video that many believe prove that the ivory-billed woodpecker is not extinct after all.

This corner of the wild South is not unknown to the elite of America's nature writers. Montana writer and wilderness advocate Rick Bass visited and wrote about the Congaree Swamp in 2003, a few years before it became a national park. Those were the days when the watery realm was still a national monument and the government wasn't trying to distance itself from calling this area a swamp. Bass toured the site with a USC English professor between a reading and class visits. He later wrote an article about his visit for *Sierra* magazine.

Bass, born in Texas, spent years working as a petroleum geologist in Mississippi. In those formative years he took long paddling trips with friends in the Smoky Mountains. It was from those outings and experiences that he wrote *Wild to the Heart* in 1987, a narrative in which he argues that you can find wildness anywhere "if you focus on the right things, and ignore the others."

On his trip to Columbia, Bass quickly tired of looking for wildness in the contemporary South's "strip malls, stop-lights, and fast food restaurants." After touring Columbia's urban areas, he commented on how "the Sunbelt's population has exploded . . . but I was astonished by all the shrapnel." In the swamp Bass walked the tourist boardwalk and called what he saw above him "a dream of light." He described particular butterflies passing and jasmine flowers spent on the water's surface. The swamp was "the antidote for civilization," he wrote.

We'd seen plenty of the spent trumpets of jasmine floating on the river, so I knew Bass had likely been here in the spring, like us. Though I had never left the South behind for the West, his ideas of wildness matched my own. I'd tried to stand witness to the explosion of human activity and look daily at Bass's "shards of wildness" embedded in our southern suburbs and towns.

This was familiar territory for Venable as well. On his late winter and spring trips back to South Carolina during the past two years he'd volunteered to ply the waters of the river swamp in a federal wildlife project to determine whether or not there was a remnant population of the ivorybills in the Congaree. In preparation Venable listened to a recording to learn the ivorybills' distinctive call and their two-note hammering on dead old-growth snags. He had floated the area that was known as their former range in the very canoe we were paddling down the Congaree but never saw or heard anything to convince him the birds had survived in their depleted habitat in South Carolina. What the search did, though, was deepen his admiration for the Congaree river swamp, and it was one of the main reasons he signed on to paddle down from Spartanburg. He said he was pleased to see the river and the river swamp as part of a vast system spanning the topographic regions of South Carolina from piedmont to coastal plain.

Rain began to fall again after lunch. We pulled out our rain gear and slipped it on. As we passed a few shabby, flood-prone cottages in a long row along the river, Venable said, "They look like Myrtle Beach come to the midlands."

In a few miles we also passed a large chemical plant set strangely in the middle of nowhere along the wilds of the Congaree. We could hear the plant before we saw it—a strange industrial keening emanating from somewhere on the west bank.

Twenty-eight years earlier, Steve Patton reported that he was lonely and tired by this point in his trip. He'd stopped on a Congaree sandbar to camp and cook rice: "I'm beginning to hate cooking for myself. I guess I'm just tired of being by myself," he wrote. He'd consoled himself that he could "chicken out at Lake Marion" if he didn't want to go all the way to the sea.

Unlike Steve, I was gaining strength. I wished we could go even farther and that the sea wasn't down there to stop our fall from Spartanburg. I looked back and imagined the six hundred vertical feet of topography between where we started and where we were on the seventh day, a hundred miles from home. The descent had seemed gradual enough except at the places where the dams had highlighted the gradient in a series of big river plugs. If I could see the elevation all at once it would be dramatic, like one of the highest cliffs in the East— or like one of the big walls that Yosemite is known for—El Capitan or Half Dome.

I had about two hundred feet left to fall in a hundred miles before I reached sea level. Already I could feel the way the hydrological energy had spread out and slowed down in the big midlands river bottoms. The power of the water was now manifest in a slow, horizontal slide downstream. The river was beginning to meander relentlessly. As we floated along we heard a turkey gobbling on the left bank. Venable mimicked the bird's familiar descending gobble and it responded in kind several times. I knew from studying the topographic maps that on both sides of the Congaree were the remainders of a much older meandering river. On maps and aerial photos I could see oxbows and graphic elegant swirls of the river's ancient journeys, what John McPhee calls the palimpsest of the former river. These changes of watery heart filled in the river bottoms—now farm fields and forest. They were a diary of courses abandoned and promises broken.

Coming around one dynamic Congaree meander, I looked deep into the flooded willows and saw what looked like the gunnels of a drowned canoe. Venable saw it too. He quickly brought us around and we paddled upstream to check it out. On closer inspection we could tell it was a green canoe, and we nosed into the willows out of the heaviest current. Slowly we pushed through and alongside the swamped boat.

"Looks like it came downstream in a flood," Venable said, leaning over to evaluate it. "One of the wooden thwarts has snapped, but it looks to be in pretty good shape otherwise."

Maybe the boat had washed down years before from someone's riverside dock upstream. Maybe some unsuspecting novice paddling in a former flood had swamped it. We felt a little like pirates. What would be the right thing to do? Leave the boat to decompose in the river, haul it out and refurbish it as a tandem reminder of our river trip, or recover it and put notices up in Columbia about a lost canoe found on the Congaree?

The river had given us a gift. To take it with us would make us part of a long tradition of river rat salvagers. We worked a half-hour bailing the old discolored canoe to get it afloat again. That worked ineffectively at best, as the old canoe kept refilling. Finally Venable jumped in waist-deep, shoved it up on a log, and rolled it over to empty it. Once we righted the boat in the sheltering willows, we could see that it was indeed river worthy. We decided to tow it downstream to U.S. 601, where Venable could haul it out and repair it. He climbed back in our canoe and we tied the battered boat to our stern. Back on the river we pulled it along like a caboose on a short train.

Late in the afternoon we reached the public wilds of Congaree National Park. Coming around a large bend in the river I began to see rectangular, white metal boundary signs nailed to trees. As Venable ruddered from the stern, I dug out my topo map. The land on river right seemed to be a tree farm of sorts with thousands of saplings in PVC pipes. The land was muddy and low and the floodwaters had washed over the saplings earlier. I figured from the shape of the bend we must have been coming up on Laurel Oaks, our park service primitive campsite that was supposed to be at the apex on the outside curve.

"If this campsite is underwater, we're screwed," Venable said as we scouted the shore for a sign. "We haven't seen any dry land for an hour."

I had already begun to lose hope we would be sleeping dry that night. We were long since soaked and the rain was falling harder. The river had risen all day, and as we floated alongside the park, we listened as the current drained away from us, through the bank trees and thickets and at all points into the river swamp. The swamp and the river had become one. North of us on the outside of the bend the river's bank was now miles away. We could float easily between the trees and within minutes find ourselves deep in the largest remaining old-growth river swamp in South Carolina. Out in the main flow we were simply paddling the mile-wide Congaree's deepest channel.

Venable spotted a picnic table on the shore in a small clearing, and we turned the canoe and ferried back across the current to a soggy landing. "This has to be it," Venable said, a hint of incredulity in his voice. "This must be our backcountry campsite."

We tied the canoes to a sapling where the old shoreline used to be and sloshed inland until we reached the rickety table. Sheet wash from the river flowed through the clearing and around the structure's legs. There was no dry land to be seen in any direction. "We could both sleep on this table," Venable said. "Or we could go downstream and hope for dry land. There's not much light left, so we need to decide."

I looked down at my arm and noticed that for the first time on the trip a squadron of mosquitoes had found my exposed flesh. "I vote for downstream."

We raised the hoods on our rain jackets and paddled through the steady downpour. Just around the bend, on the opposite bank from the park, we came upon a series of river shacks with floating docks. We talked about tying up to one of the docks, but Venable spotted some pines ahead and that gave us hope for dry land. A few hundred yards later we landed the canoes next to an old camper sitting on cinder blocks. Someone had been down to secure the place in anticipation of the high water: axes, sling blades, a weed eater, and an old lawnmower were all stacked on a high, scrap-wood table under an old aluminum carport. Inland there was a large field. In the distance through the trees we could see more planted saplings in their white PVC pipes. This area, like those we'd seen upstream, had been underwater days earlier. It didn't take Daniel Boone to notice fresh tire marks on the muddy two-track leading out.

The little camping trailer unsettled me. "We have no idea whether these guys are coming back," I said. The river was still rising. Wouldn't they return to move it?

"I don't like it anymore than you do, but I don't think anyone's coming down here tonight," Venable said. He pointed out how the two-track leading away from the riverside gained a little altitude as it snaked into a stand of pines we'd seen from the river. "I say we pull the canoes out and we take our chances."

We walked up into a patch of soggy pine straw and scouted the area. As a campsite it was marginal but probably our best chance for dry land with darkness coming on.

After we'd secured the canoes Venable inserted a stick at the water-line so we could check to see if the river was rising. While he set up our tent I heard a four wheeler in the distance. I paused and listened as the machine came closer then receded behind the ridge above us. In a half hour it would be pitch dark, and our only hope of moving farther downstream would be gone. We finished pitching our tent on our scrap of pine needles, but I was worried.

The mosquitoes were out in force, and I slathered on my first "bug dope" of the trip. The DEET-rich lotion felt greasy on my exposed arms and neck. Venable could sense I was nervous about unwanted visitors, so he lowered his powerful voice and whispered, "Sit and write. I'll start dinner."

That evening on the Congaree I confronted a healthy outbreak of David Taylor's *Deliverance* fear. Sitting in my camp chair, I wrote for a moment or two, then stared up at the treeline of pines and dark hardwoods. I strained for the sound of motors in the wet air. There'd been people in the woods earlier, four-wheeler riding, private-property-owning people. How mad would they be that two river voyagers from far upstream had sought refuge on their tree farm? I longed for the shelter of the government land across the river. "Give me your tired, your poor, your huddled masses," said the base of the Statue of Liberty. For one night we too were refugees, outcast by the flood from the nearby wildness.

I kept thinking about the irony of how vulnerable I felt camped without permission on the private land and how safe I would feel if we were simply across the river in our federally owned but fully submerged wilderness. On one side of the river the land offered refuge, and on the other, posted signs reserved the ground for single use and the limited access of private property.

In South Carolina you can legally traverse from the stream itself up to the high water line, but more than once I've had landowners challenge even that. I've been stopped midstream and told I was trespassing. Of course, there was a chance that this property owner might simply show up and bid us a good evening and safe passage in our pursuit of happiness. The landowner might admire weather-challenged canoeists for our hardy frontier ethic. As I sat there and mulled the possibilities, I wondered, if there were multiple possibilities, why was there banjo music playing in my head?

After dinner we huddled under the old carport and listened to the steady rain falling on the metal roof. I looked out at where the rising river was inching toward us about ten feet away. I couldn't hear the four-wheeler in the woods. If it was there, the engine noise had merged with the rain as quickly as it had appeared. We turned on our small electric lantern and heated water for tea and sat in our camp chairs with the light between us. It was chilly and Venable had pulled his hood up. With his long, gray beard he looked in the light of the electric lantern like an old poet, Tennyson or Whitman.

He wasn't happy we were camped on private property. Part of his apprehension, which he shared with me, was that the next day was the opening of turkey season. In spite of all this, Venable didn't seem as unsettled about the transgression as I was, and he was determined not to let it ruin his evening. His storytelling impulse kicked in. He sipped his tea and looked out at the rain. Then as if to assure me things could always get worse, he launched into a story about a backcountry plane crash a decade earlier in Alaska.

In August 1994 Venable, his brother John, his father, a friend from Spartanburg named George Graham, and Rick Whiteside, John Vermont's longtime friend, had set up a float trip in two rafts on the Togiak River in the Togiak National Wildlife Refuge, about 450 miles southwest of Anchorage. "We flew to Dillingham commercially," Venable began. "Then the five of us loaded in a Grumman Goose, a large amphibious World War II plane with a 2,200-pound payload. The put-in at Togiak Lake went fine, and we floated for a week. The plan was to take out about a hundred miles downstream.

"The take-out day was rainy and windy. We rafted down to where we thought was a good spot for the floatplane to land, took down one raft, and piled all the gear on shore, then we took the rowing frame off the other raft," Venable continued. "We were leaving the second raft inflated in case we had to float down farther. The pilot showed up in the Goose and taxied up to near our gravel bar. We asked if he wanted us to go down the river to a different spot for loading and takeoff. He answered, 'No, this should be fine, I'll pull on in and we can load as the other raft deflates.' He pulled right onto the gravel bar in the amphibious Goose and we loaded the plane. As we loaded we again asked if he was in a good place for takeoff. He said, 'Yes. Fine.'"

Before climbing into the plane Venable and his group said goodbye to a couple of refuge river rangers whom they had seen on and off that week. "Nice guys, they were doing river and camping education, checking on campsites for cleanliness. They had a motorized johnboat, which meant they could go up and down river as needed," Venable said, then broke off to slap a mosquito.

I pulled the repellant out of the red dry bag at my feet, squirted some more in my palms, and rubbed it on the back of my neck and my ears.

Most everything else was covered with clothing. I offered the tube to Venable, but he waved it away.

"Anyway," Venable continued, "the pilot taxied downriver in the plane, going slowly, like a boat, just covering some distance to leave himself a good upriver-heading takeoff. He finally turned back upstream and said, 'OK here we go.' He throttled up and the twin-engine Goose responded. We picked up speed, aiming to get to about ninety to a hundred miles per hour." As he moved into the harrowing part of his story Venable's voice got louder and louder. I looked out into the darkness, afraid the man on the four-wheeler would hear us.

"We kept going and going and going but didn't lift up. I think the load may have been too much or he just needed more straightaway, but the plane didn't climb." Venable saw the distress in my face and lowered his voice. "I was in the right front seat, pilot in the left front, and the others were in the back, seated sideways facing each other in the middle of the plane. I could see a fifteen-foot bank coming up fast and knew we were in trouble, but we were past the point of no return; that is, if he shut the engines down we couldn't stop before pitoning the bank."

Venable paused. "This was looking bad, then very bad. I yelled 'We're going to crash.' I doubt anyone heard me over the engine noise. The pilot redlined the engine and at the last second, or fraction of a second, pulled back on the wheel to lift us up. We started to rise and then BOOM, a loud noise. The next thing I knew I was sitting in my seat, dizzy, disoriented. The engines were still running, dirt and leaves were all over the windshield, which was broken, and I was bleeding like a stuck pig. I ripped off my headphones and could hear the pilot shouting, 'Get out get out, it might blow,' and people in the back were yelling, 'I'm OK I'm OK, get the door!'"

Venable said he heard a large crash—later he learned that it was from his brother, lying on his back, kicking the door out. "The pilot was shutting down all the knobs, trying to kill engine spark and gas flow. I tried to get up. I couldn't, my feet were trapped in the wreckage, where the bottom of the plane had hit the top of the bank and been crushed. I couldn't get free. I could hear the others bailing out in the back. I struggled and finally kicked loose, my wading shoes slipping off as I pulled my feet out.

"I just knew it was going to burst into flame while I was still in it, and I was wearing neoprene waders, which would melt onto my skin—a terrible way to go."

"What about your father?" I whispered.

"When I got into the back passenger compartment, there was Dad! Still in the plane!" Venable said, his voice rising again. "I thought he had gone with the others. But he had taken a pretty good whack on the head. He had Parkinson's and was seventy-five years old, so he wasn't moving too fast. I panicked again, not knowing if I could get him out, and wondering where the others were. He seemed confused and helpless, so I pushed and dragged him to the door and then pushed by him and fell out the door, four or five feet to the ground. I stood up immediately and just grabbed him, half in, half out the door, and pulled him out on top of me, and we fell to the ground. By then, John had come over and we dragged Dad away from the plane."

Venable stood up and wandered over to where he'd inserted the stick in the bank to check the level of the river. He stood there on the edge of the river and looked out into the darkness, then down at the stick. "Looks like it's leveled off. We might just make it through the night without heading downstream in the dark."

He sat back down and continued: "We were dazed and confused. As it turned out the guys in the back didn't know the crash was coming, they couldn't see out over the engine to the front, and they just assumed it was fine. They heard a big noise and saw us spinning through the air and then coming to a landing, flat, in the bushes above the river.

"We started hearing voices—it was the river rangers who had seen the whole thing and come over in their boat as quickly as they could. One of them said he could see what was going to happen and turned away. The other said he watched in horrified fascination. When we took the high-speed turn on the water, we actually hit their boat with one of the floats on the wing, and they went diving into the bushes to avoid being struck. Then as we lifted up, the tip of the left wing and the belly of the plane hit the top of the bank, both were heavily damaged, but the plane went into a flat spin, made several rotations, and then landed flat, right side up!"

Venable let out a long staccato laugh, a deep cluck, then added, "A miracle!"

✐ 601 Rendezvous

The morning of the eighth day rain fell even harder, and the Congaree was out of its banks. Hadn't we paid our outdoor adventure dues? We'd weathered rain for five of the eight days. Overnight the current had risen an inch or two on Venable's stick, but not enough to reach us and flood the tent. After breakfast we crawled back in the tent and rolled our sleeping bags and pads, then we took off our dry camp clothes and changed into our damp river gear.

Breaking camp was an exercise in patience. With the pounding rain everything had to be taken down quickly and stored in dry bags and stacked in the canoe. Out on the surface of the river I could see debris headed downstream—some cans and bottles, dismembered limbs of trees, dead leaves washed out of the backwaters of the Congaree swamp.

All morning we drifted through heavy sheets of spring rain, paddling only occasionally. In the canoe's bow I leaned back on the gear, closed my eyes, and listened to the Congaree swamp. Intricate layers of birdsong hung above the river. I heard the isolated calls of songbirds flitting in and out of the heavy willows along the inside of bends within the park—cardinals and spring warblers that I couldn't hope to identify without a book. I heard two pileated woodpeckers scissor overhead and cross the river. They laughed at us and disappeared into the dark forest when they reached the other shore. There were cliff swallows in the air above our canoe, and occasionally they'd come close enough for me to hear their wings flutter. Red-shouldered hawks whistled higher above us. There was silence too, and it was more profound because it was always punctuated with birdsong, insect thrums, and the whistle of tree frogs.

I could hear the rising river everywhere it entered the swamp on the park side. Its flow washed over low-hanging branches and swept through willows trailing in the current. As we floated past the park the punctuated swamp sounds between silences were slowly replaced with a mysterious building chorus calling from well beyond the other shore. At first it was simply an unidentifiable, rhythmic sheet of sound in the distance. Then as we cleared the river's long meander, our canoe was enclosed in a thick, thrumming mass of amphibian song. The river had narrowed, flooding through stands of willows below one-hundred-foot cliffs along the Congaree. In that flooded space at the foot of the bluffs a mass of animal life was pulsing, singing in unison as we passed—toads calling from the sloughs below the high bluffs of the two-hundred-acre Congaree Bluffs Heritage Preserve. We could see picnic tables at the top of the bluffs and the small triangular preserve signs on all the trees along the water.

What we were hearing was spadefoot toads calling by the thousands after the heavy rains. They were so loud it was as if we'd somehow paddled through a wormhole in the river and landed two hundred million years in the past in the middle of the Mesozoic. I had never heard anything like that before and may never again. The sound pursued us a quarter mile downstream.

I knew once we were past the last of the bluffs we weren't far from the U.S. 601 bridge. I was tired, wet from the continuous rain, and excited to have come so far. But I was also a little sad. What had started out in Spartanburg as an eight-day adventure with Venable was about to end. He would hand me off to Steve, and I'd close in on my now not-so-distant goal of the ocean.

Near noon we pulled over for our final lunch together. Neither of us wanted to eat in a downpour, so we singled out what looked to be an abandoned fishing shack on the left bank with a lean-to shed roof on the side nearest the river. We lowered our hooded heads and ferried across the current and paddled a few dozen yards up a flooded tributary to land in the shack's front yard. Underneath the shed it was dry and dusty, a complete contrast to the monsoon on the river. In that small shelter we ate the last of Venable's good smoked salmon and my last big oatmeal cookie. We talked about what we had seen that day. We marveled at the frogs upriver and the swift water and our good fortune finding the canoe. We talked about everything but our diminishing time together. I would miss Venable's strong presence in the stern of the canoe, even as I knew Steve would fill in with his own strengths.

After lunch the rain fell even harder as the U.S. 601 bridge came into view. The original plan had been to portage around Lake Marion. I'd arranged for Drake Perrow, a local Calhoun County farmer and Wofford alumnus, to meet us at the U.S. 601 crossing in his motorboat and haul our gear and canoe to the Lake Marion dam thirty miles downstream. That way I'd see the confluence with the Wateree River, the remnants of the Santee Swamp, and the vast lake and not feel so much like I'd cheated on my paddle to the sea. At least I'd still be in a boat. Drake's daughter Charlotte was a student of mine at Wofford, and the preceding January during a Wofford interim travel class, we'd passed through her hometown of Cameron, South Carolina. Charlotte had set up a tour of Drake's cotton gin. Making small talk at lunch I'd told him about my plan to paddle to the sea, and he insisted he'd like to help in any way he could.

But the boat trip had been called off two days earlier. Back in Columbia we'd seen a forecast for high winds and called Drake to cancel the pickup. My filmmaker friend Chris Cogan would meet us instead. I'd let him borrow my truck to haul our gear and us around the lake to where we'd put back in near Hill's Landing at the dam at the end of the lake. Chris would have a chance to add some footage to a video project he was working on called *River Time* and eliminate the complex shuttle by motorboat on the stormy lake. Drake had agreed to meet us the morning after our arrival at U.S. 601 and haul us around the dam to the put-in on the old Santee River.

Just as we approached the bridge my gray GMC pickup passed over, and Chris honked the horn to acknowledge he'd made it in time. Venable and I ferried across the flooded river toward the boat landing at the parking lot below the bridge. A concrete weir jutted out into the river. We figured that was where the landing was located and headed toward it. By the time we eddied out we could see that the parking lot was completely flooded. It looked like a lake, a lake that flowed into the spindly trees in all directions, what hydrologists call sheet flow. We sat next to the weir for a moment and looked around. A No Parking sign stood three feet deep in river water where pickup trucks with trailers for bass boats usually parked after they'd unloaded.

Confused, we took a few paddle strokes deeper into the submerged parking lot. We looked up under the bridge where the parking lot continued. There a long paved downhill drive disappeared in the water. Higher up the drive sat two familiar vehicles—Venable's teal Suburban and my gray GMC pickup. Steve Patton and Chris stood at the flood's edge dressed in rain gear. Chris had his camera out. I could see he had it dressed for the weather too: He'd snapped a little blue plastic jacket on it.

We paddled toward them, but paddling was difficult in the shallow water with the second canoe dragging behind us. I tested the bottom with my paddle. The overflowing river was only about fifteen inches deep, so Venable and I stepped out on to the solid asphalt bottom and sloshed through the water toward the camera. "I feel a little like MacArthur returning to the Philippines," Venable deadpanned, pulling the canoes along.

"Hey y'all," Chris said as we waded toward him. "Where'd you get the extra canoe?"

"Venable, looks like your canoe had a baby," Steve quipped.

Finally we were on dry land. After eight days Venable's oversized John Brown / John Muir persona handed me off to slender, muscular Steve Patton, who with his wild, electric blond hair and sparse red-blond beard looked like a true prophet lost in the wilderness. To acknowledge the handoff, Chris filmed a tag team slap between Venable and Steve.

When the festivities of arrival passed we took Louie's eighteen-foot aluminum Grumman canoe off Venable's Suburban and placed it on my truck for the drive around the lake. We replaced it with Venable's canoe and the one we'd found, then sorted gear in the pouring rain.

Soon after we were square with the leftover provisions, Venable was headed up the hill to his friend Allen's hunt camp outside the small town of Fort Motte. Turkey season had begun—and the sea was my dream, not his. I watched as he departed in the Suburban with the two canoes on top. He turned on the highway and disappeared across the U.S. 601 bridge above us. We had been together for eight days and 150 river miles. He'd been a constant presence, steering me most of the way.

When I worked at the Nantahala Outdoor Center in the eighties and nineties we'd always jokingly called the tandem canoe "the divorce boat." Unless they had plenty of practice, couples paddling canoes on moving water always ended up at odds. A canoe offers a perfect metaphoric space to test a relationship or strengthen it. Being "in the same boat" means something when the journey is long and the water is in motion, as it had been for us the past week. Venable was a good friend and we'd paddled well together. I knew I'd see him back in Spartanburg and tell him my tales of the final days paddling to the sea.

Steve, Chris, and I piled into my truck and started our thirty-mile portage around Lake Marion. I called Drake when we were on the road. He confirmed that he would meet us the next morning at a little fisherman's motel at the end of Lake Marion.

Just outside Fort Motte stands Lang Syne, the former home of novelist Julia Peterkin, the only South Carolinian to win the Pulitzer Prize in fiction. Lang Syne was once a 1,500-acre cotton plantation; it's still an active farm, but now much of it is grown up in woods used partly for a hunt club, the one Venable visited on his trips south from Alaska.

Until I researched my trip down the Congaree I didn't know much about Peterkin, in spite of her deep connections to Spartanburg. Born in Laurens County in 1880, she graduated from Spartanburg's Converse College in 1896 and also completed an MA there in 1897, less than a decade after the founding of the women's college.

After graduation she took a teaching job in Fort Motte. In 1903 she married William Peterkin, the heir to the Lang Syne plantation. The wedding was in Sumter on June 3, the same week the Pacolet River flood devastated the mill villages upstream in Spartanburg County. In fact, Peterkin's father missed the wedding because he was tending to a dozen people injured in a train wreck on the nearby Wateree River when a trestle was washed out in high water.

"The roads ran like rivers," Susan Millar Williams, Peterkin's biographer, writes. "Water spilled over ditch banks; flooded creeks swept farm animals and fences downstream. By the next morning the flood would have swept away houses and cotton mills, drowned crops and people, and washed out bridges."

Not long after arriving in Fort Motte, Julia Peterkin became the manager on her husband's plantation. That put her in close contact with African American farmhands. She was almost forty when she began to write sketches based on plantation life. She published her first book of these sketches, *Green Thursday*, in 1924.

Her most famous novel, the 1929 Pulitzer Prize–winning *Scarlet Sister Mary*, now shares literary obscurity with *Horse-Shoe Robinson*. Like Kennedy's novel it is kept in print by a university press and read mostly by graduate students in English. Peterkin's lyric prose and storytelling gift were praised by W. E. B. Du Bois and Langston Hughes, but her success was overshadowed by criticism of her style of writing African American dialect—"Keep you belly full o' victuals, make you mouth smile, laugh an' be merry if you can," says Daddy Cudjoe, a conjurer in *Scarlet Sister Mary*.

Her admirers argue that she learned to speak Gullah a patois of English and West African languages spoken by blacks in the coastal areas of South Carolina—alongside standard English, so when she began writing fiction she moved naturally into representing the speech of the black characters in that style.

When I dipped into Peterkin I looked for stories that illustrated the highly valued sense of place that southern writers are known for, but her stories and novels were strangely devoid of it. You'd think that with her plantation so close to the wilds of the Congaree that there would be a stronger sense of nature and environment in Peterkin's work, but mostly her novels and stories chronicled the human chaos. They were rich in the joys, sorrows, and travails of daily life on a southern plantation. There were complex people in her books, and they were often caught up in life's drama.

And there was plenty of the drama of nature colliding with culture at Peterkin's plantation on the bluffs above the Congaree. A 1928 hurricane took out the bridge across the river where Highway 601 now crosses. The boll weevil arrived at Lang Syne in 1917. Susan Millar Williams reports that Peterkin's husband began using pesticides to curtail the infestation. He killed not only the weevils but also Lang Syne's "birds, wild animals, and insects. They died by the hundreds and thousands, leaving an eerie silence over the once teeming fields and forests."

As we passed the turn for Lang Syne plantation I wondered whether the breeding frogs cried out in 1918 with the same fervor as when we'd passed them on the river that morning. William Peterkin's pesticide assault may have brought an early "silent spring" to the Congaree, but if it did, I was glad the silence didn't last.

✍ Lake Marion Portage

We took back roads east from U.S. Highway 601. As I drove my truck for the first time in eight days it felt strange to be behind the wheel. I'd been holding a paddle in my hands for so long. As we drove along the ridge to the south of the lake, I told Chris and Steve about finding the canoe, millions of toads calling out from the flooded swamp, the search for a dry place to sleep, and the four-wheelers in the woods. The stories were even richer telling them to others.

We were cruising along at an ungodly fifty-five miles per hour through low-country South Carolina. Even though we were on dry land, I could not forget that the lake was nearby as we drove State Highway 267 east toward the little town of Lone Star. Lake Marion is the upper lake in the vast Santee Cooper energy project, connected to lower Lake Moultrie by a six-mile-long canal. Completed in 1941, the two lakes have a combined area of over 170,000 acres. Marion is fourteen miles across at its widest. On maps the Lake Marion dam, where we were headed, was one of the most striking features of the low country, a ruler-straight line separating the blue waters of the impoundment from the marshy green swamp and remnant river downstream.

I've studied Lake Marion's reaches on maps for years. Named for Revolutionary War hero Francis Marion, the legendary "Swamp Fox," the lake is shaped appropriately enough like an eighteenth-century powder horn. We'd be portaging about thirty-three miles from U.S. 601 to the dam, and in between, the backwaters of the lake had inundated a meandering stretch of river and swamp almost twice that distance. Paddling it would have taken at least two extra days.

I felt a little sadness leaving the river behind. Before the clearing of the site for Lake Marion, the Santee had been one of the wildest stretches of river in the Southeast, "awesome in its splendor and isolation," as Walter Edgar had said in his official history of the Santee Cooper project.

As early as the 1770s engineers had dreamed of connecting the Santee and the much shorter Cooper River. The edge of the Santee River basin was thirty-five feet higher and twenty miles north, and a canal would bring ease of transportation of goods from the Santee's vast interior. Those traveling on the Santee from the backcountry would take a right turn near present-day Monk's Corner, descend through a series of locks, and enter the Cooper River basin. Through this route upcountry riverboats could unload their cargo on the docks of downtown Charleston.

The Santee Canal, run by a private company, was finally completed in 1800, and in 1801 the first farmer from above Columbia on the Broad River arrived in Charleston by way of it. Unfortunately, the canal was only profitable for two years and closed to navigation for good in 1850.

In his *History of Santee Cooper, 1934–1984*, historian Walter Edgar reports that by the early twentieth century engineers and politicians began to see in the parallel river basins potential for both navigation and electricity and began to imagine a vast project that would flood the two river drainages and create what we now know as Santee Cooper. In 1932 President Franklin Delano Roosevelt favored any scheme that would bring flood control and electricity for impoverished areas, but the first bill that would fund Santee Cooper was killed in the U.S. House of Representatives. The bill had both its champions and its enemies in South Carolina. Those in opposition thought that power production should occur only in the private sector, that poor South Carolina could not afford such a project, and that there were environmental concerns about drowning such vast stretches of river. Unfortunately, environmental concerns were not yet percolating down through the classes. Wealthy industrialists who owned plantations and hunting preserves in the river basin were the main opposition, and they didn't get their way. Julia Peterkin was among those who opposed the project. "A needless undertaking . . . to make miles of our great swamp into two enormous lakes," she wrote in a letter to a friend.

Those who favored the project claimed it would bring improved navigation between Charleston and Columbia, thereby lowering freight rates, and it would help Charleston compete with Wilmington and Savannah. Clearing the vast swamps and forests would establish, as one booster argued, "an industrial empire in a virgin land," and repopulate an area in steep decline. In 1934, to speed the project along, South Carolina established the South Carolina Public Service Authority, whose express purpose was to "develop the Santee, Cooper, and Congaree Rivers for navigation" and to "produce, distribute, and sell electric power, reclaim and drain swampy lands" and "reforest the watersheds of the state's rivers . . . and build canals, dams, and power plants, to divert the waters of the Santee." In 1935 FDR approved the project, but a group of private power companies filed suit arguing that the plan was too expensive, geologically unsound, and would do "irreparable injury" to the people of South Carolina. Santee Cooper got the go-ahead when the Supreme Court ruled in its favor on May 3, 1938.

In 1939 the clearing of the river basins began. There had been 104 million board feet of old-growth hardwood timber in the Santee basin, and another 21 million board feet of trees at least thirty years old—cypress, gum, and pine. The clearing of the basin created a vast public works project. Walter Edgar reports that nine thousand were employed in logging alone. The work wasn't easy or painless, as it displaced the population settled in the two river basins. The lakes' construction created a vast rural renewal project, with 1,100 tracts of private land bought or condemned by eminent domain for a total of 177,000 acres. Over nine hundred families were resettled outside the basins of the lakes. Some houses, schools, and churches were moved, and others were rebuilt.

In *Sunken Plantations*, a sort of alternative story to the official company history, Douglas W. Bostick traces the locations and histories of twenty historic plantations drowned beneath the waters of Marion and Moultrie. Some of the plantation houses were emptied and dismantled before the rising waters claimed them. Others were simply abandoned. The story of Pond Bluff Plantation on the Santee Swamp would prove the saddest of all the losses. Pond Bluff was near the town of Eutaw Springs on the south side of Lake Marion a few miles above the dam. The first house on the property was built in 1773 by the namesake of the lake, the Swamp Fox himself. When Marion died in 1795 he left Pond Bluff to his wife, and upon her death, the house was supposed to pass to his grandnephew on the condition that he change his surname to Marion. The will was not properly executed, and the property passed to other heirs after the death of Marion's wife. The house burned in 1816.

In 1825 another house was built at Pond Bluff, this time by the Simons family. The last heir, Joseph Simons, refused to sell it in 1939 when Santee Cooper demanded the property. Simons fought the seizure until all his legal options were exhausted. Bostick reports that on July 7, 1939, after the utility company seized the plantation through eminent domain, Simons entered the house, placed a pistol to his temple, and took his own life. Simons, a casualty in the battle for the upper

Santee, is buried at the Rocks Cemetery on an island in the middle of Lake Marion.

By the time we bypassed the lake it had become a legend in my mind, like the Swamp Fox. The legend was built on the stories I'd heard from Steve about his trip across it and on the sad history of the construction. I could feel the lake's presence as we drove on the ridge above it. I felt a little guilty for abandoning the river, even though the actual river had been lost for sixty years below the waters of the lake. I told this to Steve and Chris, and Steve told me to get over it. "I've paddled it, John," he said, "and Lake Marion is a canoe ordeal."

With my exit from the river I had now parted ways with earlier River Voyageurs. In 1981 Steve Patton had paddled across the lake, and in 1969 Doc Stober's flotilla of canoes had paddled it too, entering the lake from the Wateree River. Once they were in open waters they'd lashed their boats together and paddled a shortcut that a game warden in a canoe showed them through the lake's upper end, still known as the Santee Swamp. They'd camped on high ground above the lake about two miles below the I-95 bridge. After dark they sat around the campfire and heard stories of a local legendary Santee Swamp character called Moss Man, a sort of redneck Sasquatch who looked like he was covered with Spanish moss. That night two of the Wofford boys decided they wanted to sleep in a cave along the bank of the lake. "Moss Man appeared and made believers of the cave-dwellers . . . two wide-eyed and shaky lads . . . began to wonder if cave living was a good idea."

The River Voyageurs continued to paddle Lake Marion the next day and then they headed into Lake Moultrie. Their account shows no conflicted reflections about the lakes. They simply accepted these impoundments as realities they had to encounter and cross. I had hoped for some discussion of the lakes and the vast, historic Santee Cooper project, but the log of the River Voyageurs made up with humor and personal detail what it lacked in history and reflection.

When the River Voyageurs turned toward Charleston, my narrative and theirs parted paths entirely and would never merge again. They paddled down the diversion canal, across Lake Moultrie, and through the locks into the basin of the Cooper River. Three and a half days later the River Voyageurs landed in Charleston and closed their educational adventure. They stayed in a barracks and visited the naval base. They toured a minesweeper. "The Navy treated us like the sailors that we were," the log of the River Voyageurs records on the last page.

The story was very different in Steve Patton's journal. Besides being tired, Steve was very lonely by the time he'd reached the upper reaches of Lake Marion on the ninth day after he'd left Pacolet. "I'll never be a hermit," he wrote. "Independence is ideal but seclusion stinks." Steve called the swampy back reaches of the lake "the sea of anticipation" and paddled through it all afternoon. Finally, in early evening, he'd come to the open water of the lake. "It was almost dark, and even careless youth was no excuse to head into a situation like that." With the lake ahead of him he started paddling back upstream toward the last dry land he'd seen. As luck would have it, Steve encountered a fisherman headed back to Santee State Park for the night who towed Steve's canoe to a campsite. "I got to talk to someone," a melancholy Steve said at the end of the entry for that day. Paddling the lake took him a day and a half more because of a headwind. As he paddled across the lake he lost confidence, "lost in the elements that drive me toward the ocean."

East of U.S. Highway 601 the lake widened and deepened and no bridges crossed it until I-95 fifteen miles east. As we drove along that rural road, signs for boat landings were at every intersection. Every one of them made me think of Venable and Zubie's friend Hobie Buffington.

Across the lake and just north of our route was where Hobie had set up his catfishing business and where Zubie had watched him throw his depth finder in the lake. We headed down the rural highway to the end of the lake, or the beginning, depending on your point of view. We drove to the hamlet of Eadytown near the dam, where Steve and I got a motel room alongside the diversion canal and waited for Drake's assistance the next morning.

The earthen dam on the Santee is 8 miles long and it has a 3,400-foot spillway with sixty-two gates for flood control. In 1941 the last spillway closed and the lake filled to full pool with the waters of the Santee River. After the completion of the Marion and Moultrie dams most of the river system's annual flow was retained in the vast lakes connected by a diversion canal or was flushed down the Cooper River to the Charleston Harbor. An unintended consequence of the project was the negative impact on both the Cooper and Santee rivers below the dams. As little as five hundred cubic feet of water per second was released into the remaining fifty miles of the old Santee riverbed. Writing in 1956, Henry Savage said the lower stretches of the Santee "became an abandoned river." The waterway also became much saltier because ocean tides in the lower river overwhelmed its meager flow and pushed upstream.

In spite of optimistic predictions, sediment loads in the Cooper River increased, causing dredging costs in Charleston Harbor to climb dramatically—and ironically—given that increased water flows were supposed to scour the harbor. In the 1980s, the Army Corps of Engineers built yet another canal, this one an expensive rediversion canal to channel water back into the Santee, attempting to mitigate the problems they'd caused forty years earlier.

Rerouting a river as if it were an irrigation canal is not often simple or successful. In the long run, the forces of nature complicate the best human solutions. I learned about this from reading John McPhee on the complex engineering problems of the lower Mississippi that he explores in *The Control of Nature*. Engineers in South Carolina underestimated the Santee River in the 1930s and 1940s, and many people believe they underestimated it again in the 1980s with their so-called rediversion canal. Both projects were executed at great costs, financial and otherwise, to the American public.

I was glad Steve had given me permission to skip Lake Marion. Was it a copout? An adventure-paddling cheat? I had set out to paddle the rivers of South Carolina, not a huge man-made impoundment that was a product of political and social forces of the 1930s. For me, Lake Marion was an engineering monstrosity and it held no attraction. Maybe it's a fault in my humanities training that I don't have much fascination with modern human engineering. A single mile of wild Santee River could hold my interest longer than the biggest artificial river impoundment in the world. A man-made lake is a mere placeholder, a clot in a natural system that over time will clear itself. An impoundment is simply waiting for centuries and gravity to release the flowing water from our utility or recreational needs and return it to the natural river it once was. On the Santee, time will prove more powerful than politics and engineering.

~ Hill's Landing

Besides a concrete boat ramp at Hill's Landing there's a restaurant, a
ten-room motel, and a small concrete building for cleaning fish. Some
might call it a fishing resort, but Steve took one look at the complex of
buildings and christened it the "bo-tel," as in boat hotel.

We parked the truck in the gravel parking lot and bolted through the
continuing downpour for the restaurant door to rent a room. A TV sat
on an old table in a corner; it was tuned to the Weather Channel. The
front was moving fast. "Clear skies by tomorrow," I told Steve.

"But there are wind advisories on the lake," the waitress added as she
passed with a plate.

Three men were eating late lunches in the restaurant. I picked up the
menu—mostly burgers and fried fish. Every plate came with frozen,
machine-cut french fries and sweet slaw. It was the kind of place where
ranch and thousand island are the dressings of choice. No one asks for
balsamic vinaigrette.

Chris was headed back to Murrell's Inlet on the coast, so at the
checkout counter I reserved a twenty-dollar room for the night for
Steve and me, passing on the thirty-dollar option, which included a TV.
We got the key from the guy on duty, and Chris bought a six-pack of
Budweiser for us to drink as a before-dinner cocktail.

We drove to the back of the property through puddles in the gravel. The ten motel rooms were in a line, like single-wide trailers framed in with plywood and rough-cut lumber. There was a concrete slab in front of each one, protected by a flimsy porch roof.

For an hour or so Steve, Chris, and I sat on the front porch of the Hill's Landing bo-tel, drank beer, and talked over the logistics for the rest of the trip. Chris had rented a small, aluminum skiff in Murrell's Inlet and he and another filmmaker, Tom Byers, planned to motor up-river to meet us above U.S. 17 on the last morning to film our approach to the sea. Chris was anxious about how he and Tom would make contact with us on the final day. Cell phone service was spotty, and we might simply disappear into the Santee River heart of darkness. How were they to find us on the final day?

Steve sipped his beer and studied our set of topo maps spread out on the stained concrete porch. He did some calculations of time and distance, tearing off a corner of the beer holder and using it for a ruler. "If everything goes according to schedule we'll camp our last night a few miles above the U.S. 17 bridge," Steve said. "And we'll arrive at the bridge midmorning on Sunday."

Chris had brought a coastal chart for the Georgetown area. He spread it out too. "I talked to a friend who knows the Santee Delta well, and he suggests we enter the ocean on the South Santee rather than the North," Chris said, tapping on the chart. "The inlet for the south branch of the river is sheltered and will give us some protection if there's bad weather."

"You can get some good footage upriver," Steve said.

"I want a dramatic approach shot of the canoe with the marsh be-hind it after you've passed under U.S. 17," Chris explained. "This is where we'll set up the camera." He pointed to a small island about a mile below the bridge on the South Santee. "That's where we'll see you for sure on the final day."

We agreed. Once we'd found Chris and Tom we would continue down the South Santee channel together to the sea.

"Sounds like a plan," I said, cracking open a second beer.

"Once we cross under U.S. 17, we'll have ten miles to go," Steve added. "We need to keep the tides in mind."

High tide was at 6:14 on Sunday morning, and low tide was at 1:23 p.m. If we wanted assistance from nature, we could ride the tide all the way to the ocean. But if we were late, we might have to enlist Tom and Chris's skiff to pull us out. That would make for an ignominious end to our trip.

Steve told Chris how the river channels could be a little confusing upstream. Below Jamestown, where U.S. 17-41 crosses, the Santee is pretty straight for ten or fifteen miles, then it wiggles through three or four major meanders and splits into the North Santee and the South Santee, where Wadmacon Creek comes in from the north. "The intersection where the branches split is not marked, and it's hard to keep your bearings," Steve warned. "If we somehow end up on the North Santee we won't know until we see the U.S. 17 bridge and the boat landing there."

"We'll take our chances," Chris said, "and maybe we'll have contact by cell before we get to U.S. 17."

After finishing his beer Chris headed back to Murrell's Inlet, leaving Steve and me to relax on the front stoop of the bo-tel. All our talk about the sea made it clear that this was really going to happen. We were within striking distance of the coast. We drank the last of the beer, and Steve cooked a stir-fry on the camp stove. After dinner I walked a garbage bag full of wet gear to the front office, where the manager at Hill's Landing was nice enough to dry all my clothes.

As we finished dinner a black man pulled up in an old blue beater pickup and started unloading a bed full of catfish with a coal shovel.

He pushed two wheelbarrows full of fish to the wire-walled cleaning shack hanging over the canal and disappeared inside. We walked over and stepped in, introduced ourselves, and talked as he cleaned the fish.

He was tall with a salt-and-pepper beard and a camouflage hunting cap. His blue work shirt had "O.J." stitched over the pocket. He tied on a black apron and pulled a yellow-and-blue plastic glove on his left hand.

O.J.'s lilting low-country accent was like something Julia Peterkin might have tried to capture in dialect. I'd never heard anything like it before. It sounded Caribbean. It took me a minute or two to adjust to his rhythms of speech. He said he'd worked on the Santee Cooper lakes as a fishing guide for twenty-four years.

The catfish in the wheelbarrows were stiff with rigor mortis. O.J. pointed to each species with his filet knife and called out their names. "Channels, blues," he said. "Flatheads, bullheads." The cats all had black whiskers and pink, dead eyes. Some were a sickly green, some white, and others a wet, oily black. O.J. pointed at two of them he said were close to thirty pounds.

He seemed happy to have the company and wasn't surprised when we told him we were headed to the sea the next day in a canoe. He said he'd always wanted to do that himself. As we watched he pulled three or four cats out of the wheelbarrows by the tail and piled the day's catch along the back edge of the wooden counter covered with plastic cutting boards. Then he went to work with the knives.

O.J. sliced with speed and accuracy. He slapped the wet, leathery cats on the white plastic and filleted each fish in less than a minute, the creamy pink flesh sliding along the thin, curved blade of the ancient knife. The carcasses and guts went into white pickle buckets on the floor. He said he filleted two wheelbarrows full of fish every day and left the catfish steaks for that day's fishing clients in the Hill's Landing freezer.

Once O.J. started working, a chorus of white egrets showed up, waiting out front for handouts.

"Do you clean other fish besides catfish," I asked.

"Black crappie, redbreast, largemouth and striped bass. They used to be some good striped bass fishing, but that's long gone. We might see a striped bass once every two weeks." He tossed a handful of catfish scraps to the egrets in front of the shack, and they hopped into place to devour them.

"And what about the rest of the guts and carcasses?"

"Used to throw it in the canal, but now I load the buckets in the back of my truck every day. I got me a backhoe at home and I bury 'em. I dig a new trench every day and move the garden around the yard. These cats grow some good eating collards."

I thought of how Squanto was supposed to have taught the Pilgrims to bury a fish in each mound of corn. O.J. went well beyond that wisdom with his backhoe.

That half-hour watching O.J. cleave catfish flesh from bone was like a little fossil encounter with an older South. He seemed more deeply grounded in his place than anyone else I'd met on the river trip so far. Sitting back on the porch Steve remarked how much he liked the rhythms of O.J.'s speech. "I stood in the shack and listened to the music as much as to what he had to say."

That night we drank Gatorade since the beer was long gone. It had finally stopped raining, and in the foggy, filtered light we watched the last of the day's fishing charters come up the diversion canal. Right next to us a truck hauling a big bass boat backed in, and two hefty fishermen stepped out and stretched.

"How's fishing?" Steve asked.

"Sucks," one man said as his friend unloaded their cooler. "The power company's dropped the lake two damn feet because of all that water coming down from upstate. We're going somewhere else tomorrow. You boys know anything about Lake Wateree?"

"I know where it is," Steve said.

"Well, we know that too," the man said.

The man walked back and plugged their boat into an outlet above the porch to charge its onboard batteries. He pulled over a hose and cleaned the hull. Their boat was a sight to behold: It was a high-dollar bass rig, a baby-blue twenty-one-foot Ranger with 225-horsepower engine, trolling motor, and a high-back pedestal seat in the front. I guessed it must have cost forty thousand dollars.

After the two disgruntled fishermen walked over to get some dinner, Steve pointed out how if we turned ninety degrees, in the distance behind us on Lake Moultrie we could see the steam plume from one of the Santee Cooper electric plants against the clearing sky to the east, "finally blowing the other direction."

Looking at the steam plumes reminded me that these lakes provided power for the people of South Carolina. Some had called the project a white elephant. Even Henry Savage had dismissed it as a Depression-era "pump priming program." He claimed that despite the project's supporters "painting glowing pictures of the industrial progress which the development would bring to the low country," little would come of it. Though barge traffic to the midlands was cited as a major reason for drowning the upper Santee River, there turned out to be almost no shipping between Charleston and Columbia after the system was built, and by the time the project was completed, "hydroelectric plants had become almost as passé as inland navigation" and coal-fired electric plants were providing most of South Carolina's power.

So what good was Lake Marion? At the time of Savage's writing he claimed that the largest artificial lake in the east was merely a "fishpond," but as a fishpond, he admitted, it was "unsurpassed." Savage would say that for sixty years fishermen like O.J. have reaped the biggest benefit from the huge project. As I remembered Savage's protests I thought of the days before Santee Cooper when there still would have been people cleaning fish at the end of the day, but they'd have been doing it by lamplight.

⟜ Our Bridge Too Far

The morning of the ninth day, Steve and I walked over to the restaurant for an early breakfast. The sky overhead was clear to the west. Inside the dining room there was sportfishing frenzy in the air. Large men filled the tables. They had a defined mission for the day: Catch fish. Two waitresses rushed by with platters of eggs, sausage, and gravy biscuits. The air smelled like weak coffee and boxes of loam in the worm cooler. Lacy condensation fogged the windows facing out on the diversion canal.

The TV on the old table in the corner was still tuned to the Weather Channel, just as it had been the night before. All the anglers glanced at the screen between their bites of eggs and grits to get a taste of what their day on the lake might bring. As I had already gathered from looking at the sky, the front had indeed moved through over night, but the TV's crawling text at the bottom told me what I knew from common sense: Wind would follow.

Standing at the register waiting on a table I read a South Carolina Department of Natural Resources sign taped above the Peppermint Patties: "Unlawful to take striped bass under 26 inches from lower Santee System." A map defined the system so that there was no ambiguity. The river system stretched along the route I'd descended from the Columbia diversion dam on the Broad River, the Lake Wateree dam on the Wateree River, and the Lake Murray Dam on the Saluda all the way to the beginnings of the Santee Delta. "That's half the state," Steve said. "At least the fishermen have to do some thinking about river systems. That's more than most people in cities do."

Striper fishing is a top-of-the-food-chain pastime for the sportsmen who congregate on the Santee lakes. The striped bass is the South Carolina state fish, sometimes called rock fish. Their streamlined, silvery bodies are marked with longitudinal dark stripes running from behind the gills to the base of their tails. They can be monsters: 6 feet long, weighing 125 pounds. Fish biologists think that the fish can live thirty years.

Like shad, stripers spawn in freshwater, but they naturally spend most of their lives at sea. Almost all the rivers of the Atlantic Seaboard once had striper breeding populations. Only a few remain. There are also a few spawning populations of landlocked striped bass, including the one in Lake Marion. But the southern striper fishing on Lake Marion is not what it used to be, and there are many theories out there as to why. Scientists say the decline could be due to pollution, siltation, construction of power dams, and overfishing.

The intellectual exercise of reading about declining populations of anadromous fish—that is, fish that run up rivers to spawn—and about the science of striper fishing holds some interest for me, but the pure on-the-water fishing part never has. I look out over the tables and shake my head in bemusement and tell Steve, "This is not my tribe."

"Catch 'em, clean 'em, and cook 'em—that's the Garden of Eden most of these guys are looking for," Steve says with his own level of amusement.

Steve had more grounding in the world of fishing than I did. In his youth he often fished with Venable's younger brother John. Before we left for our paddle to the sea, Venable had passed on a clipping from the Spartanburg paper from the 1970s showing the two proud boys holding a large carp they'd caught at a local lake. Steve had laughed at the picture, saying that John and Venable's father, Bunn, actually helped land the big carp, but the paper didn't need to know that.

We three paddling friends form a complex continuum, with Venable's love of sportfishing / river recreation at one end, Steve in the middle with less sportfishing and more recreation, and me on the other end with no fishing and lots of recreation. The missing elements of our continuum (out on the edge past Venable) were these off-the-chart sports fishermen eating breakfast at Hill's Landing. They were the pure, low-country hook-and-bullet crowd with limited engagement with conservation unless it impacted whatever species they wanted to hook. They were mostly purists, intent on, as Steve put it, landing, cleaning, and cooking.

Two of the fishermen finally left and we sat down. I sampled the conversations around me as I looked at the menu, and I heard what might as well have been a foreign language. At the table nearest the door, two unbelievably fat men in camouflage were talking about "crappie jigs" and "three-pound leads." Across from them two thin-faced men leaned into their coffee cups and bad-mouthed the power company for dropping the lakes and ruining their fishing.

"I've heard, 'If you love South Carolina's wild places and wild animals, thank a hunter or angler,'" I said to Steve as I glanced around the dining room.

"I don't know exactly what that means," Steve said quizzically.

"The argument's entirely economic. The fees and taxes these hunters and anglers pay fund some of the state's conservation efforts. Thirty-five years ago in South Carolina it probably would have been true, but today people who say that should also thank the land trusts, DHEC."

"And the Nature Conservancy, the Audubon Society, and the state park system and many others," Steve added, catching on.

The waitress took our order. "I'm not willing to accept that these guys are entirely responsible for all my state's wildness," I said.

Drake Perrow arrived at Hill's Landing at about eight thirty in his silver pickup with a toolbox in the bed. He'd hitched up a utility trailer to haul our canoe and gear to the Santee River boat landing below the Lake Marion dam. Drake was dressed casually in khakis, a blue pullover, and a maroon cap. He was happy to see us and apologetic that the boat shuttle had not worked out the day before. There was a hint of the same lyrical low-country cadences we'd heard in the voice of O.J. the catfish cleaner.

The drive to the landing didn't take long, but along the way Drake told us about how he maintained one of the oldest family farms in America. Their place near Fort Motte had been under cultivation since a king's grant in the early 1700s. The Perrows were directly related to Fort Motte's most famous resident, plantation matron Julia Peterkin.

"Was Perrow a Huguenot name?" I asked, hoping it would be, a nice tie-in for me with the lower Santee settlement of Jamestown we'd pass the next day.

To my disappointment Drake said it was not. His king's grant ancestors who settled the land near Fort Motte had been English, as the upper reaches of the Santee were called "the English Santee." His Santee ancestors had married into the Perrow family a hundred years later. "That Perrow was originally from Maryland," he said.

At the boat landing Drake backed near the water, and we unloaded and quickly began packing our canoe for the trip downstream. Upstream, partially shielded by trees, we heard the flush of the discharge clearly as the backed-up river was released. The dam was a backdrop in the distance. A number of the sixty-seven floodgates appeared to be open, but not enough to significantly raise the water level. In spite of all that rushing water the river still seemed low and slow compared to the Congaree two days before. Lake Marion's giant powder horn was taking in all the excess floodwaters from the upcountry.

Two women were sitting on pickle buckets along the river's edge, wetting hooks and using spinning reels. One was white and one black. This was local subsistence fishing, not the high-dollar, boat-driven sport we'd witnessed back at Hill's Landing. I smiled at them and they smiled back as I walked up to the top of the boat ramp to get a picture of Drake's rig. I saw more DNR striper posters stapled on trees, but this time locals had spray-painted the cellophane-covered posters expressing their inhospitable feelings about the government. We were back on the frontier.

We packed the canoe on the edge of the boat ramp. Louie's Grumman had lots more room than Venable's Dagger, and I felt odd stowing my bags below the gunnels. We'd always been packed high in Venable's boat. "What's with the dog food bag?" I asked as Steve transferred his gear to the canoe.

"Trash bag," he said, picking up the empty bag. "I brought it from home. I'm just recycling."

A half hour and a dozen tight meanders later we lost the sound of the lake water pounding through the open floodgates out of Lake Marion. The territory on that side of the Lake Marion dam didn't conjure the best memories for Steve. On his first paddle to the sea he'd fought the wind as he crossed the lake. He'd headed for Randolph's Landing at the lake's north end. At the landing a man had hauled his canoe around the north end of the dam. Steve carried his boat downstream and put in on the lower end of the dam in what he found out later was a borrow pit, a long, marshy pit used to borrow dirt to build the earthen dam. "I thought the pit had be connected to the Santee River," he wrote in his journal. "But when I got to the end of it I found a big dike between me and the river."

He had put two holes in his boat portaging and had been hassled by a wildlife officer (the land around the borrow pit is state game land and off-limits). He had just enough time before the sun set to patch the holes, and he ended up camping that night next to the borrow pit.

Our first few miles down the old Santee, we made slow progress, but there was plenty of wildlife to keep us entertained. We saw eagles, ospreys, and anhingas. We also saw two flocks of five or six great blue herons. That was a first for me, as I had only seen these impressive stoic wading birds foraging alone on upcountry streams.

That first day paddling together we found a rhythm. Steve was in the stern and I was in the bow. I'd look back from time to time and admire Steve's classic J-stroke. With each stroke, Steve's top hand ended with his wrist bent forward and his thumb pointing down at the water. The stroke is essential for crossing lakes in high winds, digging hard for each inch of forward momentum, but it's also the most efficient way to move a canoe down a river. Seen from above, the path of the paddle traces a J shape in the water.

A few miles from the landing we startled an eight-foot alligator, and it scrambled into the water from a nearby exposed mud bank. In quick succession we saw three more, and Steve altered an old drinking song—"A hundred gators asleep on the bank, a hundred gators asleep. One slides in and we're nervous again, ninety-nine gators asleep on the bank. . . ."

We'd been told in the restaurant that shad were in the river, and we'd see people fishing for them. The cashier had said there was one shoally spot between the dam and Highway 41. "Y'all be careful there," he said. "That's where the shad spawn, and the water can be real swift for a canoe."

Steve remembered the shoals. In 1981 a drought had left the water so low and slow that he'd actually seen the rocks in the riverbed: "It was so shallow I had to get out and pull the canoe over the rocks."

Venable had told me about the shoals too. Once he'd been turkey hunting on the Santee and had put in with a friend well below where we were. They'd motored upstream and he'd discovered the shoally spot too. But if the rocky area was there, we didn't see it that morning. The water was high enough to wash out features on the bottom, and we saw only a few fishermen.

Steve reflected on the Santee Cooper project and the diverting of the river. "It seems a tremendous feat to channel a river out of its bed and send the water somewhere else," he mused. "And to a higher degree it seems a ridiculous feat. But who am I to talk? Paddling three hundred miles alone is even more ridiculous."

By late morning the river's meandering seemed endless. We figured we were covering only two or two and a half miles each hour. "At this rate it might take us a day and a half to get to Highway 52," Steve noted with some concern. "And it's almost as long again to where the rediversion canal dumps back into the river."

"Not good," I said. I was beginning to add up the hours remaining before we reached the sea. Perhaps I had miscalculated. For the first time in nine days my well-conceived schedule felt threatened, and I had a sudden sinking feeling. I worried that due to the many meanders I could have underestimated the paddling time from the Lake Marion dam to the ocean by as much as two days. Back in Spartanburg I had measured the distance with a string laid on the map, but apparently the string could not accurately mirror the distance. Steve had suggested that my schedule was ambitious. I had just chosen to ignore the truth.

I brooded in the front of the canoe. There was no way I could add two extra days to the trip—by Tuesday morning at the latest I was due back at school in Spartanburg. When a gator splashed into the river I didn't sing Steve's alligator song, and I didn't notice much else either. I had come so far and I wasn't going to make it.

At lunch I reeled out a strip of my dental floss and I knotted each end. I pulled out the beat-up set of *Gazetteer* topo maps. We were on map 8 with only three left to go to reach the sea. I laid the knotted end of the string on the landing where Drake Perrow had dropped us in the river below the Lake Marion dam, and I followed the meandering route of the river with the floss to the Highway 52 bridge and then on to the confluence with the Santee Cooper rediversion canal north of the town of St. Stephen.

Without a GPS, it was impossible to know exactly how far we'd paddled in three hours. There were no road or rail crossings between the dam and Highway 52 to measure our progress against. We knew from the map and from our experience that the river had doubled back and forth on itself. I measured the map as the crow flies, and from boat landing to canal it was eight inches. That was a little over nineteen miles. Not so bad. Then I carefully and slowly fit the floss to the tiny meandering riverbed. Then I stretched the string out straight and measured it against the scale at bottom of the map—"1 inch = 2.4 miles or 3.8 km." I did the calculations and was stunned to find out it was forty-four river miles to the rediversion canal.

"If we've made ten river miles so far we're lucky. At two miles an hour we've got a helluva long way to go," I said, my enthusiasm deflated. I understood now why so many the nineteenth-century engineers dug canals between tight meanders on large, navigable rivers. The Santee River seemed endless, and for a moment I longed for a few more canals to speed the trip along. I felt helpless, almost as helpless as I had on the side of the Rio Reventazón in Costa Rica.

Steve tried to make me feel better: "By the time I'd reached this far on the Santee, I'd lost energy too."

That summer in 1981 Steve's father had given him a plywood and fiberglass canoe. Gibbes was a botanist with a PhD from Yale. I studied botany under him at Wofford College in the early seventies. Gibbes was one of the early biologists in the Southeast who was interested in ecology. Before he came to Wofford he helped establish the arboretum at the University of Alabama. Gibbes was legendary in town for his early ecological vision and perseverance when it came to water issues. Over the years he wrote so many letters to editors, agencies, and individuals to express his concern for environmental matters that his missives acquired the nickname Gibbs Grams.

Steve's mother, Connor, was an early computer programmer, and when I returned to Wofford College in the late eighties, she was running the college's first computer lab there. The youngest of four children, Steve had two brothers, Buzz and Reed, and a sister, Charlotte. Buzz had been a good friend of mine in high school and college. I knew Charlotte because she had worked at Wofford as a comptroller. I'd somehow never met Reed, though I knew that he worked in a factory in Spartanburg.

I've always thought it was odd that I didn't know Steve growing up. Spartanburg was a small enough town back then. I had connections to almost everybody else in the family. Our five years difference in age kept us apart.

"I wanted to be a farmer or a carpenter back then," Steve said. "People who knew my parents would say, 'Oh no, Steve shouldn't do that. He has to get a good job because both his parents are so well educated.'"

By 1977 when Steve was in the twelfth grade, he knew college wasn't right for him. The first year after high school, he worked odd jobs, but his father convinced him it would do no harm to apply to college. At his father's insistence he applied to Eckerd College in St. Petersburg, Florida, and he received a scholarship and enrolled.

Steve enjoyed Eckerd in the fall of 1978 and the spring of 1979. He thought about being an art major. A general education professor in a humanities course, "an old fellow, very reserved," made him think about things in new ways.

There were good friends there too. "I still keep up with a guy named Rich who was a marine biology major," Steve said as we paddled through another meander. "He's worked with techniques to kill mos-quito larvae without pesticides."

What Steve remembered most fondly about his year of college was paddling in a canoe out to an island in Edward's Bay, an arm of Tampa Bay. "That was the end of the seventies, you know. So I smoked dope in the mangroves and stared up at the clouds."

The year after he graduated from high school his oldest brother, Buzz, transferred from Wofford to the University of Southern California in Los Angeles. Buzz joined some kind of a religious group there.

After spring semester was over, Steve hitchhiked to Los Angeles to see his brother. By that time Buzz had graduated from USC and was working part-time in a bike shop out there. Buzz had also joined Sun Myung Moon's Unification Church.

Steve stayed out in California three months trying to convince his brother to come back home with him. Meanwhile, he took a job in a marina cleaning boat hulls. When his brother moved to San Francisco, Steve followed, sleeping on couches and working odd jobs.

"In my view of things, had it not been for my brother joining the Moonies, I might have settled into four productive years at Eckerd College," Steve said wistfully. He never went back to college.

In 1981 Steve gave up on convincing Buzz to come back to South Carolina and returned to Spartanburg. That's when he decided to pad-dle to the sea. He asked his dad if he could borrow the plywood and fiberglass canoe.

In his journal Steve reflected about years traveling: "I've been traveling every time I got the chance and I've almost always gone alone. I've gotten to know myself pretty well in that time but there are a whole lot of other people in the world I'd like to know."

When I read Steve's journal, I thought of Thoreau's *Walden* and the famous assertion in the first chapter, "I should not talk so much about myself if there were anybody else whom I knew as well." Thinking momentarily of *Walden*, I wondered if Steve realized that our trip was much more like one of Thoreau's lesser-known classics, *A Week on the Concord and Merrimack Rivers*, in which Henry David and his brother John work their way upstream from home in 1839. Thoreau's narrative, like mine, is built on the days of the week, the voyage progressing with each day. The book is an adventure story, a travel narrative, and a digressive essay on many topics, including friendship. There is also a shadow of tragedy inherent in the river voyage as well: Thoreau's brother John contracted lockjaw and died three years later, leaving Thoreau to stock the narrative, when it was finally published in 1849, with references to lost people and places.

Steve seemed to have matured beyond Thoreau, and I was hoping I had as well. Maybe that trip alone settled Steve down. A few years after he returned from his paddling trip, he married his high school friend Penni and started a lawn care and landscaping business. He'd made peace with his brother's past choices.

Steve's always been a great paddling companion, and he brought me out of my funk as I listened to him compare his 1981 river with the Santee River we paddled today. "In 1981 the old riverbank looked more like a sandbar at the beach. The old river must have been twenty or thirty feet wider before the original diversion when the dam was built. The river was very shallow back then, and you could walk all the way across."

The river continued to meander ceaselessly back and forth, first north, and then south, as if we were paddling along the coils of a rope.

We took to calling the Santee "the Endless River," and our goal, State Highway 52, "our Bridge Too Far."

We knew we needed to camp well beyond the Highway 52 bridge in order to have any chance of making the rediversion canal by noon on day ten. We both knew there was a good chance that the current in the river would pick up once we made the canal, but would it pick up enough to make up lost time on our trip to the sea?

I tried not to think about the problems of logistics and whether we'd meet the filmmakers at the sea in time. I tried to concentrate on the meandering river, the occasional osprey or great blue heron, and the river's banks slipping past. In order to break the monotony I switched up with Steve and paddled stern for a few miles. Sitting in the stern was a rare feeling, and I wasn't sure I liked it. I was so used to my role as second mate. Paddling stern complicated things.

Paddling positions in a canoe can lend themselves to deep metaphorical significance. *Stern*, by related meanings, suggests seriousness, hardness. The position is where much of the steering takes place, and the position at the rear is always the heart of the boat's forward movement. To bow is to submit, to yield. That's what you do when you choose to paddle up front. It's also to bend—and, spelled the same but pronounced slightly differently, it's an instrument that can propel an arrow forward.

I like being a bowman. I like the view, but it's deeper than that. It's psychological: I have reluctance to lead. On the river I like being in a position where I'm not the expert, the one in charge of the trip or someone else's life. That's why I took to the kayak so quickly. I would have made a good Eskimo. In a kayak I can always be in charge of my own destiny. I am one with the boat. In a canoe you're married to the other paddler. There are vows—"Thou shalt not paddle but on one side at a time," and "Thou shalt keep to the chosen path."

Like a marriage, there are sharply defined commitments and lasting responsibilities.

I did fine with my new position in the stern though, and I settled into the rhythm of paddling and holding our course. I left a little of the blues behind, not thinking so much about our destination downstream. There wasn't much I could do to improve our time. I focused on practicing my J-stroke. I worked on turning my thumb and the top hand away from my body, causing the blade to angle slightly away from the canoe. I tried to make as little sound and wake as possible. My stroke wasn't as practiced and crafted as Steve's, but I was beginning to feel what a good stern paddle feels like. I was moving us downstream efficiently.

About this time we came around a bend and saw the elusive Highway 52 bridge in the distance ahead of us, our Bridge Too Far. We were not stuck forever in a meandering hell through the South Carolina lowcountry wilds! We'd been paddling ten hours and dusk was upon us. As we approached the modern concrete bridge a dozen black men and women were fishing along the shore. They sat on pickle buckets with their rods propped with fork sticks in the sand. They waved as we passed, and we waved back.

We stopped to rest a few minutes at the boat landing on the far side of the Highway 52 bridge. We pulled out the water bottles and drained them and then looked at the *Gazetteer* topo maps from my map case. We'd moved from map 8 to map 9 once we'd made the bridge, and that gave me a feeling of cartographical accomplishment. Achievement or not, I knew we still had a long way to go. We could not linger at the Highway 52 bridge. Steve figured we had about an hour until sundown, and we needed to get as far downstream as the light would allow.

Still we dallied to chat with a skinny old Santee fisherman in a blue work shirt, jeans, and a Dixie Bait cap. He was O.J. the catfish skinner's pale downriver twin. We had landed the canoe next to his camouflaged johnboat, where making room for him, we waited to one side for his fishing partner to drive the trailer down the ramp. We watched as a middle-aged woman backed the trailer wheel deep into the river.

"Any luck?" Steve asked, looking into the man's boat.

"Been out all day with my daughter. She's the one backing the truck. We got three roe shad and a herring to show."

I asked to see the shad and he reached in his cooler, pulling out a three-pound silver fish with a V-shaped tail. "The founding fish," I said, quoting the title of a John McPhee book, a love song to shad and shad fishing. "Finally I can add a sighting to my life list."

Steve asked about the herring.

The old man put the shad back in the cooler and pulled out a smaller fish, holding it up with a finger in the gill. "That's what you buy smoked in them little boxes. The shad roe is good, but this herring roe is really fine fried in cornmeal."

I hoped he'd keep talking. His accent rivaled that of O.J. back at Hill's Landing.

The old man's daughter stepped out of the truck and introduced herself. "Where'd y'all come from?" she asked.

We told her the simple story, how we'd come down from the Lake Marion dam and how we were headed for the sea.

"It's nice to finally see some water in the river," she said. "I'm sure that's helping y'all out some. Last year it was terrible out here with the drought."

She said she'd been as far as the U.S. 17 bridge fishing with her father but had never been all the way to the sea.

Steve asked what else they'd caught fishing on the Santee. She thought for a moment and said, "One year Daddy caught a flounder all the way up here." She spoke as if this was a common fact of the river, something to be expected, though we were still over fifty miles from the sea. The flounder story was our first hint that the ocean was nearby.

We might yet get there if we just continued to put one canoe stroke in after another. If a flounder could do it, we could.

We watched the old man load his boat on the trailer as he'd done hundreds of times before. He climbed in the truck cab, drove the truck forward, and the trailer pulled out of the river one more time headed for the parking lot. When her father was out of earshot, his daughter smiled. "I been coming down to fish with him for years when the shad are in the river. I know he won't be around much longer. He loves to fish. He's eighty-four, and his health is slipping. I'm not sure I'll come back here after he's gone."

That evening we paddled another two miles downstream and set up camp on the river's north bank deep in the Santee Swamp, still not sure we had enough time to make it to the sea. It was eight p.m. by the time we landed, and there wasn't much light left, but at least we had no rain. The sky was clear and dark blue at sunset, at least what little we could see through the trees above the river.

As we were setting up the tent, we noticed three surprised wild hogs watching from about fifteen feet away. I clapped my hands, and they realized we weren't friendly visitors and bolted for the deeper woods. In the last of the light I could see hog droppings on the ground all around us. We had set up camp on a hog interstate. If they would stay away for the evening, I'd be happy to give them back their forage ground in the morning.

Steve cooked spinach and cheese burritos over the camp stove. The food lifted my spirits a little. Soon after we made camp, we heard a train crossing the river and we were able to place our campsite exactly on our map. The news was bad. We had a long way to go and we were way short of where we'd planned to camp. What we heard in the distance was the CSX freight line headed for the rail yard at St. Stephen.

As I listened to the train I thought again of Henry David Thoreau. Thoreau spent two years and two months at Walden within earshot of a train. "The machine in the garden," historian Leo Marx calls Thoreau's experience of enduring the onslaught of the Industrial Revolution. We were two hundred years on down the line, and the trains were still interrupting our reverie. This one would trouble my sleep with horns and clanking boxcars through the night.

As I tried to get to sleep I sorted through our options like a man serving time. We had no choice but to stay with our plan, no matter how many hours it took to get downstream. I'd started the morning full of energy and expectation, thinking that paddling down the old Santee to the sea would be easy. Instead this had been the darkest day on the river.

There was one chance left: If the current picked up considerably after the confluence with the rediversion canal we might make the sea by Sunday afternoon. I didn't have much hope though. The day of dead water had done me in and it seemed the distance was too great. If there was good cell phone service at Jamestown I would call off the meeting with the filmmakers. At this pace we'd never meet them Sunday morning on the South Santee for the filming of our triumphant final push to the sea. Maybe we'd just take out at the Highway 17 bridge, ten miles shy of our goal, as Steve had in 1981.

Right before sleep another train passed, and I was glad for its presence. I found it comforting on a day I needed reassurance. In a weak moment I thought that if I gave up entirely I could simply hop a freight train like Woody Guthrie and hobo back to Spartanburg in a day or two. Trains, unlike rivers, go both ways.

⌒ The Lower Santee

I woke to a mix of train sounds and coyote howls. The coyote chatter, familiar sounds from behind my house in the piedmont, made me homesick, made me miss Betsy and our morning rituals. I wanted to rise early and sit alone at my desk and write, drink coffee, and read the local paper. I'd woken up in a tent in a different place every morning for ten days, and I was ready to be grounded again. I was ready to leave my J-stroke behind and make a beeline for home. I'd had a boat under me for 10 days, I'd traveled 240 miles, and I was ready to stop moving.

On the river there's the illusion that you're moving steadily forward, so there's not much prompting you to look back or regret. It's only when you pause like we did to camp overnight that the doubts pool around you. The "what ifs" fill you like a flood. Well, I told myself as I stuffed my sleeping bag away for the tenth time, *We're not doing what-ifs today. Today I'm paddling toward the sea, just like I said I would.*

I put out of my mind the knotted string of floss in the map case and the distance left to go and my worries over the shifting tides. Generations of coyotes had come thousands of miles in their migrations east. Surely I could hold it together for two more days. We live in a strange world when coyote howling can make a southerner like me homesick and confident at the same time.

We were on the river by eight with the lower Santee all to ourselves. My confidence waned again as I felt the new day's first mile settle into my shoulders and back. I stared blankly at the bank passing by. I'd lost interest in birds. We couldn't make the canoe go any faster, and I knew if we continued to make less than three miles an hour it would be another long day like the one before, and by evening I'd be deeply depressed. I focused on the hope that the rediversion canal would add significant current to the river. If we could make Jamestown by early evening we'd have a better sense of how much farther we could go on Sunday. All I could do was paddle and hope for the best.

The morning passed quickly. Nearing noon we floated up on two fishermen in a fancy bass boat. "Had any luck?" Steve asked as we pulled even with them.

"Water levels screwed," the older man said, sitting in the high swivel seat at the front of the boat.

"They keep dropping that damn lake," the younger one said from the boat's rear. "And we ain't catching shit down here."

"Way too much water," the older one said.

This was our chance to get a read on where we were. "How far are we from the rediversion canal?" Steve asked.

"About two miles," the older man said, casting into the current.

That meant at worst we were about an hour from the rediversion canal, where we would discover whether there was any possibility of reaching the ocean by Sunday. I was cautiously hopeful.

"Daddy says fishing was always good before that damn canal," the younger man said, nodding toward the man in the boat with him.

"Fishing was real good," his father agreed. "I don't know exactly what they did, but the striper fishing's gone."

"It was that damn canal," the younger man repeated emphatically. "That canal screwed the striper runs to holy hell."

We paddled lightly to stay even with their anchored boat. The older man began to reel out his own version of an impressive lowcountry conspiracy theory.

"You know they got all that government money," he said about the contractors. "They dug that hole way back in there without no roads. When they finished that canal they left all that heavy equipment up in there. The government had paid for it. Just buried it and filled up the ditch. There's dozers and earthmovers buried all down in there. They just left it all in there because they got all that government money. I flew over it once and you could see them all down in there. One day they were there, and the next they covered them up in dirt. I tried to get the pictures for the paper, but they wouldn't run it. I'm in construction. You think I could afford to bury a D-9 dozer?"

The theory seemed harebrained to me but typical of South Carolina storytelling. It was time to move on.

"I may be naive, but I don't sit around and fabricate theories about what our government's trying to do today to screw up my world," I said to Steve as we paddled downstream from the bass fishermen. "In my experience it's mostly private greed or collective stupidity that screws things up, not institutions."

Steve laughed and told me that my worldview was fine but not everyone in the watershed shared it. "My neighbor Donnie is convinced that our weather is screwed up because power companies are experimenting with wind power in the Midwest. 'It's them big fans they're making electricity with,' Donnie says. No matter how much you argue with him. He still believes it's the big fans."

Around noon we began to notice the river rising. The current strangely looked like it was now running upstream. Paddling suddenly became more difficult. "This must be the backwash from the rediversion canal," Steve conjectured.

Soon the river changed color, grew darker as it contained more suspended sediment of the upcountry, and picked up speed. Then the landscape opened up, the river widened, and we finally entered the joined waters of the old Santee and the rediversion canal, bringing flow from Lakes Marion and Moultrie.

Steve ruddered us downstream, and our canoe took off like a shot. I placed my paddle across my lap and leaned back and closed my eyes. I felt the velocity of the current pick up and I let the waters carry me away. A minute later I glanced at the faraway north bank. The river was twice as wide as before, and the sea didn't seem so far away. I caught a glimpse of what the old Santee might have looked like before the big dam was put in upstream. "We're going eight miles an hour, maybe more," I said in disbelief. "We're finally riding the flood again."

At that rate we could possibly make it to Jamestown by late afternoon. If we had to we could camp there on dry land near the bridge, or we could take our chances and head on downstream. We both knew that if we wanted to meet up with the filmmakers and make the sea by Sunday afternoon it would probably be important to push on, but we didn't talk about possibilities as we rode the flood downstream. We simply enjoyed gravity's free ride. We wanted to see how far and fast it would push us.

We passed miles of flooded Santee swamp forest and an occasional abandoned hunting camp. Steve commented on how much smaller the trees looked this time around. We wondered if this insight was the result of a heavy logging rotation, the destruction of Hurricane Hugo in 1989, or simply a trick of memory. Things often seem bigger in the remembered past after we revisit them in the present.

The water rushed out of the riverbed all along the way and into the swamp, filled with dark, young cypress trees. I looked for signs of the outgoing tide too, but it was hard to distinguish it from the rushing flood. Steve had seen signs of tide that far inland in 1981, but he was paddling through a dry spring and there wasn't a rediversion canal yet; the tide was really all there was to raise or lower the river levels back then. We knew we'd have the tide with us at some point, but with the floods pushing downstream from upstate we had all the watery propulsion we needed.

I felt like Huck Finn riding the big river. All along the Santee I'd sensed the freedom Twain's fictional character had had on the Mississippi, but I like to think Steve and I weren't running from demons as Huck Finn was. We were 150 years further down the literary line, and "civilization" had smoothed some of our edges over time. Unlike Huck, we were both middle-aged. We had mates who trusted that we weren't lighting out for the territories but for the sea—eleven days away, where people from Spartanburg take their one-week vacations at the beach in July and August—and that we'd return home as soon as we got there. Hell of a thing, civilization.

◡ *Jamestown Landing*

The lower Santee is still sometimes called the French Santee. Resilient French Huguenots with names such as Huger, Gervais, Poinsett, and Mannigalt settled it in the seventeenth century, and for almost a hundred years they had their own peaceable kingdom up the Santee River. In the 1800s they spread throughout the society of early South Carolina, taking part in public office, and civic and economic affairs. Arthur H. Hirsch in *The Huguenots of Colonial South Carolina* claims that by late 1777 when the French adventurer and soldier Marquis de Lafayette visited the state, the Huguenots as a cultural group had become "so completely a part of the province . . . as to become one with it." A few still worshipped in French in Charleston, but mostly "they were one with the English."

In *River of the Carolinas*, Henry Savage describes how the French society along the lower Santee formed around wine, olive oil, and silk in the seventeenth and eighteenth centuries. The Huguenots transformed "this remote forest wilderness into a garden spot unequaled in America." Savage had a deep affection for the Huguenots and the civilizing effect their culture brought to the lower Santee. He called theirs "a society the grace and elegance of which were perhaps unsurpassed." He backs up his admiration of the French settlers with listings of Huguenot heroes in the South Carolina colony: brave soldiers such as Francis Marion and Peter Gaillard; tidewater farmers and inventers such as Peter Jacob Guerrand and Gideon Du Pont; merchants such as Lewis Timothy, editor of the *South Carolina Gazette*; and early industrialist William Mellichamp, who developed the first large-scale salt-production plant in the lower South. Savage ends his chapter on the Huguenots saying, "The great river flows now by desolate swamp and lonely forest; but the influence of the Huguenots remains a vital presence in the life stream of the Carolinas and the South."

In 1700 the English explorer John Lawson led a small expedition out of Charleston, traveled up the Santee River, and visited the Huguenots on the French Santee only ten years after they'd settled the area. When he arrived the river was flooding, and to Lawson, "the Woods seem like some great Lake, except here and there was a Knoll of high Land which appeared above the Water." Lawson's expedition made its way up the Santee by oar boat and his party stayed several nights with the Huguenots. Lawson noted that the Huguenot settlers still traveled the wide river mostly by large dugout canoes, though the settlers were not a great distance from the mouth of the river. In later years small sailing ships would come up the Santee as far as Jamestown. Lawson says the river "fetches its first Rise from the Mountains and continues a Current some hundreds of miles ere it disgorges itself, having no sound, bay, or Sand-Banks." In his journal Lawson also mentions the "repeated Freshes" (floods) that had often covered the floodplain. On the day Steve and I paddled toward Jamestown we could see one of Lawson's "freshes" all around us.

Now the productive farms and plantations that once lined the Santee are no more. The Huguenot names are spread throughout the state; Greenville has its Poinsett Highway and Spartanburg its DuPre House and Marion Avenue. There's even a singer in my hometown named

Fayssoux. Few hear these names of upcountry places and think of the lower Santee, but they should. Henry Savage certainly would.

Around four p.m. we pulled up at the Jamestown concrete boat landing at a bridge known as Alternate U.S. 17. There was little in the view from the boat landing to suggest that the Huguenots and their rich civilization had ever been there. If there had been a town at the crossing it had vanished as surely as Grindal Shoals and Pinckneyville.

We felt some relief because we'd arrived with plenty of daylight ahead of us. After a brief rest we could continue a few hours downstream and set up camp before dark. Steve looked at the maps, did a quick calculation, and figured we'd averaged about eight and a half miles an hour from the rediversion canal to Jamestown, quite an improvement over the day before. We celebrated with a Gatorade and pulled out the dental floss to calculate our final distance to the sea.

The river was a pretty straight shot to the coast from Jamestown. We stretched out the string in a straight line along the lower Santee and calculated that it was 25.2 miles as the crow flies from Jamestown to the sea, and we figured in extra distance for one patch of meanders.

Our next task was to contact Chris and report on our progress. We had not talked with him since he left us at Hill's Landing on Thursday night. I retrieved my cell phone from the dry bag and powered up. Amazingly, I had service. I punched in Chris's number and left the heart of darkness of the Santee Swamp behind. He picked up right away. "Where are y'all?" he asked.

"The Jamestown boat landing."

"They're at the Jamestown landing on the river," Chris said to someone in the background. "Jamestown? How far is *that*?"

I heard laughter in the background.

"Where are you?" I asked.

"I'm in a little store somewhere deep in the Francis Marion National Forest, just driving around," Chris said. "Hey, they know Venable out here, and they say I'm only fifteen minutes away."

I walked up to the large parking area at the top of the boat landing. There were four or five trucks with trailers parked in the shade, fishermen upstream for the day. Closer to the river there was an old beat-up Toyota pickup with rust holes in the fenders. Next to it was a Harley. Two women and a man leaned against the pickup and eyed me cautiously. They looked like bit players for an apocalyptic movie.

I walked back and sat on the canoe to wait for Chris. I finished my Gatorade while Steve pored over the map. Before long, we heard Chris honking the truck horn as he approached from the Georgetown County side of the river. He parked near the ramp, unloaded the tripod, and hauled the big dry box with the camera in it down from the truck. All the while, the scruffy threesome watched his every move. Chris had a huge smile on his face. He dropped the tripod and case to the ground as we walked up, and he gave us both high fives.

"This is amazing," Chris said, launching into his encounter at the county store. "I was just out driving up the river and I found this store on a gravel road in the forest. I thought I was lost, so I stopped and went inside. I asked for directions, and they asked what I was doing, and I starting blabbing about you guys paddling to the sea, and this guy in camouflage says, 'I got a hunting buddy named Venable Vermont doing that same thing.'"

Anxious about time, I told Chris we needed to get going if he wanted to shoot any footage. "For us to get to the sea on schedule we'll have to get another six or seven miles before dark," I said.

Chris cranked into high gear, quickly set up the camera. "Hey, no problem. You'll be back on the water in fifteen minutes."

The two women and the man from the parking lot walked down to the riverside, drawn by Chris and the video camera like birds to a feeder. They looked to be in their late thirties. One woman wore a camouflage halter top and blue jeans. She had silver studs in her face. The top of her hips and her stomach rolled appreciably over a wide belt. The other woman, the Harley rider, was slim. She wore a little black pillbox hat with silver studs in it and black leather chaps over her jeans and black boots. The man was dressed like an aging frat boy lost in the Santee wilds—gray cargo shorts, an Old Navy yellow tee, and a red Rebel Yell cap. These were no Huguenots.

The three stood back and watched as Chris set up the tripod. They seemed nervous, and their eyes ranged around as if they were worried about what might happen next. They looked high to me.

Chris worked on camera angles. He checked the direction and intensity of the light. He set up the shot he wanted with us in the canoe and the bridge behind us. I grew more concerned when our gallery walked a little closer and Cargo Shorts asked, "What are y'all doing?"

"Y'all must be turkey hunting," Biker Woman said.

"No," Steve said, matter-of-factly, "we're just floating, headed down to the ocean."

"In a canoe?" Studs-in-Her-Face asked.

"You need a motor to go that far," Biker Woman said. "That's a hundred miles."

"Not quite that far," I said, busying myself with the canoe, hoping they'd go away.

"You can get to the ocean from here in a canoe?" Studs-in-Her-Face asked Steve. "I been coming here for years and I never knew that."

"We figure we got about thirty miles to go," Steve said, trying to be friendly. "We'll camp somewhere downstream."

"A canoe is something we don't see much here at this boat landing,"

Studs-in-Her-Face said. "Mostly fishing boats and game wardens. Sometimes a county cop."

"Where y'all from?" Steve asked. Steve would talk to anybody.

"Charleston," Biker Woman said. "But we been up at Georgetown at the flea market."

"What's that camera for?" Cargo Shorts asked.

"He's making a movie," Steve said.

"Hi, y'all," Chris said, looking through the viewfinder on the camera, focused on setting up the shot with us and the canoe. He waved distractedly.

"How much that camera cost?" Cargo Shorts asked.

"About twenty thousand dollars," Chris said. I swallowed hard.

"Damn," Studs-in-Her-Face said.

"You ought to sell some pictures of them going down the river to the Charleston TV station," Cargo Pants volunteered. "They'd give you six hundred dollars."

"I'm not a reporter," Chris said. "I'm making a movie. I'll just wait and use it in that."

"Six hundred dollars is nothing to sneeze at," Cargo Pants said. "You ought to see some of the crap makes it on the news. They'd like this. Man, this is human interest."

"Hey, y'all are going to have to be quiet for a few minutes," Chris said. "I'm getting ready to roll here."

Chris turned on the camera. He asked us questions about the trip since he'd last seen us. Our boat ramp audience soon lost interest and wandered up toward the pickup, where one by one they crawled in the cab.

"Chris, stop the camera a minute," I whispered. "I'd be careful telling those three how much your camera cost."

"You mean they might rob us?" he asked, not clued in at all.

"You heard what they said about the flea market. I think they're up there getting high right now." I nodded my head toward their truck.

"Damn," Chris said, looking back over his shoulder at the pickup. "I got to be more careful."

"I don't want you hanging around to get B-roll of us leaving the ramp," I instructed. "You need to leave before we do and get the hell out of here with that camera."

"Damn," he said, even more excitement in his voice. "This is dangerous."

"You go. We'll be fine," Steve said.

"Let me finish up," Chris said.

Five minutes later Studs-in-Her-Face and Cargo Pants staggered back down the ramp from the truck. Biker Woman reappeared too, rearranging her nose. They walked over to where Chris was shooting and assumed their spots in the gallery.

On camera, we talked about how the whole trip looked in jeopardy on Friday but how once we made the rediversion canal our spirits brightened. "We thought all was lost," I joked. "It was indeed a 'heart of darkness.'"

We were sitting in the canoe and had our paddles in our hands, and Chris had us framed with the river behind us.

"OK, I got some good things," Chris said, finishing up. "What's it look like for tomorrow? Are y'all back on schedule?"

"I think so. If you guys get an early start in the johnboat, motor up the South Santee. If not, we'll meet at that point below the U.S. 17 bridge where you said you wanted to film."

Chris glanced back over his shoulder at the gallery, and then he unscrewed the camera from the tripod. "Y'all be careful," he said. "I'll see you tomorrow."

"You want some help carrying that to the truck?" Cargo Shorts asked.

"Naw, I got it," Chris said, swinging the sticks over his shoulder. "Y'all have a good day."

Chris hightailed it up the hill to the truck. Cargo Shorts watched, disappointment seemingly burning through the chemical haze in his brain as the twenty-thousand-dollar camera disappeared into the pickup.

After Chris left, I finally relaxed. Once the distraction of the expensive equipment was gone the three observers were sincerely fascinated with our canoe and gear.

"Hey, I got a question," Studs-in-Her-Face said. "What you got dog food with you for?"

Steve laughed. "It's our trash bag."

She seemed to take this in stride, and then it was Biker Woman's turn. "What do y'all do for a living?"

"I do yard work," Steve said. "And John here, he's a professor on spring break."

"A professor?" Cargo Pants said, stepping back. He thought for a moment. "You got all kinds of cars. Why you want to paddle a canoe all the way down here?"

We pushed on. Not far from the bridge, we passed a large isolated yellow buoy cabled in the current. Rusted and battered, it looked as if it had been abandoned for years. I couldn't quite figure out its use but I glanced back at it until it disappeared behind us in the distance. For me it was a concrete symbol for our proximity to the sea and a sign we just might make it after all.

Eight miles downstream we set up camp on a big bend on the edge of the final map from the *Gazetteer*. Steve hacked a flat place for the tent and pulled the boat on shore for the night. "We're gonna have a right pretty sunset," Steve said. On the inside of the bend the river was still flooding into the low forest. Below us it disappeared, headed for the not-so-distant sea.

❧ Aiming for Hampton Plantation

On the final morning, Steve did some more calculations. He laid the floss along the river one more time. "Twenty miles to go." Then he added up the mileage from the day before—"33.6 river miles," the longest river day of the trip. With the water from the rediversion canal pushing us along we'd averaged over five miles an hour. Steve walked down to the river and checked a stick he'd placed in the ground at the high water line. "The river is up this morning," he called back to me. "We'll still have the advantage of the release through the canal, plus we're well within the tidal range. That will help push us along too."

As Steve packed and cleaned up, I studied the trip maps one final time. I flipped through the sheaf of damp pages from the *South Carolina Gazetteer* and marveled at how far I'd come. When Ron blessed the boat on day one, Venable and I were almost within sight of the Appalachian Mountains. On the first map, contours defined the hilly piedmont landscape, sometimes as tightly bunched as a fingerprint. As Venable and I had traveled east the land loosened up and spread out. In Columbia we left behind the last of the hard country rock and entered the territory of softer stones—limestone, sandstone—laid down in horizontal beds by the action of wind and water. Finally, on the last map, half the space was covered with the flat, blue, inky reaches of the Atlantic.

The cartographical coastline of South Carolina bulged outward below Georgetown where the Santee River entered the sea. There was little solid land and no elevation. Just to the north of the Santee, the Great
Pee Dee, Black, and Waccamaw rivers flushed directly into Winyah
Bay, all in a ten-mile stretch of Carolina coast. Where we were headed,
millions of years of sediment transportation from the eroding upcountry had built one of the biggest river deltas on the Atlantic Coast. All
along the Carolina coast there were barrier islands and inlets, but this
stretch was different. On my map the delta islands were vast swirls of
silt deposited by the meandering rivers, suspended in time, stalled only
by the cartographer's craft.

I followed the river downstream. Human history was a veneer
thin as ink in the delta. There was little beach development from
Georgetown to Charleston, and the names of the old rice plantations still lingered next to the vast system of ancient rivers, marshes,
and creeks—Esterville, Annondale, Rice Hope, Kinloch, Cat Island,
Wedge, Harrietta, Hampton.

For fifty miles south, most of the vast delta plume was owned by
the state or federal government (Tom Yawkey Wildlife Center Heritage
Preserve, Santee Coastal Reserve Wildlife Management Area, Cape
Romain National Wildlife Refuge) or held in trust by the descendants
of rich industrialists who still hunted and fished along the coast on
vast preserves.

As I surveyed the map I zeroed in on Hampton Plantation, the ancestral home of Archibald Rutledge, the long-dead poet laureate of
South Carolina and distant relative of Steve's by marriage. Hampton,
the stark white Georgian-style mansion, was originally built in the
1740s. Today it is preserved and open to the public as part of Hampton
Plantation State Historic Site. We would pass the creek that led to it
later that day.

The plantation was one of South Carolina's richest historic sites, with a history going back to the early Huguenot days. It was one of the spots where humans grabbed hold of the shifting delta and held on with all their might. In 1744 Daniel Horry purchased six hundred acres from Anthony Bonneau and built the original house. The plantation would eventually encompass several thousand acres, much of it cultivated rice fields, a crop that would yield unimaginable wealth for a few in low-country South Carolina.

The Huguenots first harvested silk, grapes for wine, and olives for oil, but after a few decades they replaced these crops with rice and indigo. Rice, grown in South Carolina as early as the 1680s, evolved from an upland crop to a swamp-grown crop when a method of cultivation was developed that allowed it to grow in standing water. Thousands of acres of lowland marsh in Georgetown and Charleston counties were suddenly very valuable. In the mid-1700s rice land doubled in value every three or four years, and by the eighteenth century rice was South Carolina's leading export. Rice was to South Carolina, as historian Walter Edgar says, what sugar was to the West Indies and tobacco to the Chesapeake.

In 1768 Daniel Huger Horry, the grandson of Daniel Horry, married Harriott Pinckney, the daughter of Charles Pinckney, former governor of South Carolina and a signer of the Constitution, and moved her to the plantation. The British targeted the house during the American Revolution, as it was a known refuge for Patriot friends, including Harriott's mother, Eliza Lucas Pinckney.

The first time the British visited they were looking for Francis Marion, who had stopped off at Hampton for provisions. The Swamp Fox swam across the creek and hid in the rice fields while the house was searched, and he evaded capture. On their second visit, the British were looking for Daniel Huger Horry and Major Thomas Pinckney. Pinckney escaped, but Horry surrendered and pledged his loyalty to the Crown. The raiders took valuables but left the house standing. When the war ended the Horry family restored the plantation to its glory. The plantation then passed into the Rutledge line when Daniel and Harriott Horry's daughter, Harriott, married Frederick Rutledge in 1793. The plantation was still in the Rutledge family when Archibald was born there ninety years later in 1883.

I'd always hoped that we could approach Hampton from the river and that we'd have enough time on the journey to pay homage to the poet and conservationist in his home place. That morning, looking at the time and the distance we still had to cover, a stop at Hampton seemed unlikely.

I asked Steve to tell me what he remembered about Rutledge. "When I knew him he was about as old as God," Steve said, "and I was younger than the devil."

In the 1960s Rutledge spent the summers in the cooler climate of the upcountry. Steve's dad would take him and his brothers to see the famous writer on Sundays after church at Aunt Camilla's house on Alabama Street in downtown Spartanburg. Rutledge had been married to Steve's aunt's sister. "We'd work in the yard," Steve said. "Camilla would serve us lunch and we'd listen to Archie tell stories. Dad knew Archie was a living storybook, and to us boys all those stories were true."

Rutledge wrote more than fifty books, but he's probably remembered mostly for his hunting and fishing stories about the lower Santee and Hampton Plantation. He wrote often for the popular outdoor magazines of his time and won the prestigious Burroughs Medal in 1930 for his book *Peace in the Heart*, an honor he shares with Aldo Leopold, Rachel Carson, Barry Lopez, and other writers of natural history prose.

Though Rutledge served as South Carolina's first poet laureate from 1934 until his death in 1973, his reputation as a poet hasn't held up well against the changing tastes of the contemporary literary world.

Deep River, Rutledge's collected poems, came out in 1960, but it's now out of print.

I could tell Steve enjoyed talking about Rutledge. In fact, the idea of paddling from Spartanburg to Archie's ancestral land on the Santee had been a big motivational force behind Steve's first trip to the sea, but even he'd never made it all the way to Hampton. On his last night on the river in 1981, not far from where we'd spent the night, Steve had slept on a sandy beach of a small island, about ten feet from the water's edge. When he went to sleep the river was low, and he neglected to tie his canoe. "After a few hours I woke with water around my feet," he wrote in his journal. "Half-conscious and dreaming a little, I thought I was going down the river in the canoe." He groped around and realized he wasn't in his canoe but was wrapped in a wet blanket. "My canoe was gone. Left without me. The tide had risen overnight and flooded out my campsite."

He started walking the shore of the island in the dark looking for what he called "my lost love." Maybe it had snagged on a log or a sandbar. "Before I got far I was ankle deep in water and realized my island was a big sandbar with trees on it. Not seeing the canoe, and not knowing what else I could do before daylight, I found the highest spot I could and I waited to see how much of my island would sink."

At dawn he found he was on a three-foot-wide strip of sand. He stripped off his clothes to keep them dry and he slept. When he awoke he saw what he thought was his canoe—something long and skinny along the shore—and swam the river to retrieve it.

"As I got closer, the object turned out to be a log. I saw something else and swam to what turned out to be another log."

Steve was in despair by this time. He carried his clothes and gear from the island to the bank, where he dressed and began to walk up the riverbank back toward Jamestown and the last bridge he'd paddled under. He flagged down a fisherman and explained what had happened. "I was ready to offer him all forty-three of my dollars and my left ear to go downstream and look for her, but he cheerfully refused any compensation for the rescue."

They found the canoe about two miles downstream, floating on the river with everything inside completely dry. "New rule of thumb," Steve wrote in his journal. "Always pull the canoe out to the level where you are sleeping and tie it up."

Steve didn't find Hampton Plantation that day. He missed it because of wind, tides, and the misfortune with the canoe. Losing the canoe ended up being the culminating event of his epic trip, the crowning story. The next day he abandoned his quest for the sea ten miles short at the U.S. 17 bridge. Watching Steve assess the distance left for us to cover that morning, I realized that making it to the sea might be very important for him, maybe even more important than it was for me.

Nearby, the bold river sluiced past. Outside the perimeter of the camp saplings enclosed and protected us like a palisade. As we had struggled through the endless meanders upstream, I had been the one who lost faith, and Steve had assured me that we'd either make it on schedule or not. There wasn't much we could do but paddle. The plan had been mine. I had set up an eleven-day trip and we had acted it out to its culmination. Now Steve seemed to have taken on the role of navigator, and I sensed that his confidence was growing that we could achieve our goal.

⌐ Atonement

By 8:30 a.m. on the eleventh day we'd struck camp, packed the canoe for what I hoped was a final time, and entered the swift current at the outside of the bend in the river. From the stern Steve powered us out from shore but in the process lost his straw hat on the rough branch of a willow. We watched as the hat hit the water, swirled once, and disappeared. Good omen, or bad—Steve wasn't interested in superstitions. He just wanted his hat back. For a hundred yards he guided us through a game of hide-and-seek as he spotted the hat just under the surface, rolling with the current. We never caught it, and the hat finally vanished for good.

We made good time in the series of meanders above Hampton Plantation. As we paddled through each switchback I watched the shore for some sign of where the North and South Santee rivers parted ways. We were approaching one of the wildest reaches on the Atlantic Seaboard, finally paddling across the last of nine topos from the *Gazetteer*. Months earlier I'd drawn a circle around a series of three distinct inland meanders near the map's left margin, at the parting of the North and South Santee. This area was where we'd always feared we would take a wrong turn and end up in the north branch of the river rather than the south.

Two years earlier, scouting for this eventual trip, Steve and I had driven down to the lower Santee for a quick down-and-back paddle to check out the stretch of the river above U.S. 17. That August we arrived in the deep afternoon and camped in Francis Marion National Forest, surrounded by live oaks, slash and loblolly pines. We were the only ones in the wilderness campsite save two men whom Steve called "national forest gypsies" who'd been camping there for weeks, foraging in the forest for edible mushrooms. A smoky fire kept the mosquitoes at bay that night, and at dusk a great horned owl hunted around the edges of the campground.

The next morning we had paddled several miles from a Forest Service boat landing down Wambaw Creek to the South Santee. On the way to the confluence with the Santee River, five or six small alligators had slipped down pluff-mud banks into the water as we passed. Night herons were roosting in the cypress. By the time we reached the South Santee I felt we were alone with the current and the sky.

Paddling back upstream to the boat landing, we encountered the king of alligators floating silently along in the middle of the creek. Its head was as wide as two canoe paddles, and we estimated from the size of its head that it was ten feet long. When the regal reptile finally decided to submerge, the surging wake bounced our canoe like a whitewater flume. I'd seen plenty of alligators, but I was always surprised by how impressive a big one could be.

We saw no alligators on the lower Santee on this trip. The river was still high, and any place where a gator could bask was swamped under three feet of muddy, surging current. All around us the river siphoned into the cypress swamp and emerged on the opposite side of each meander. You can get lost in such a watery landscape. We kept to the channel and felt pretty confident we were where we wanted to be—in the South Santee headed for our midmorning rendezvous with Chris and Tom, who planned to put a johnboat in the north branch then head up the south branch to meet us. Several times we heard a motorboat in the distance then watched as it approached and passed with no film-makers at the helm.

Finally we began seeing docks and dead yellow marsh grass, indica-tions that we were getting close to the sea. At one point we heard shoot-ing in the woods, and I said, "Sounds like the Battle of Wambaw Creek." Though we joked about it, we never saw the confluence of Wambaw Creek, and that should have been our first sign that we'd missed the South Santee. We kept paddling and finally saw the big highway bridge. We paddled underneath and I said, "I wonder if they are lost."

"No, I think we're lost," Steve said. "This is the Highway 17 bridge boat landing." He pointed up the ramp to the parking lot. "And that's your truck. We're on the North Santee."

We didn't have time to be lost. With the tide turning at midafternoon there wasn't room for mistakes. I crossed my paddle on my lap, pulled the map out of the plastic case, and stared down at the hard truth. With my finger, I followed the North Santee upstream to where we must have taken a bad turn. The troublesome meanders jumped up at me from the printed surface like a snarl of rope. I knew all along it had been there where we lost our way. The schedule we'd made earlier seemed doomed again. I put away the map, dropped my paddle back in the water, leaned forward in my seat, sighed, and stroked a few times to pull us alongside the boat dock.

At high noon we ate our last two oranges, some crackers, and a tin of smoked oysters we'd been saving until we could smell the sea. Next to us a middle-aged man in Docksides and a blue Hawaiian shirt loaded a small skiff, preparing for an outing. His wife stood off to the side watching as he carried the last of the gear from the car.

"Where'd you come down from?" she asked.

"Spartanburg," I said, feeling smug. "Eleven days."

"Oh, I did that trip in 1974," the man said, walking up. "I went to Furman. Spring break our senior year, a buddy and me canoed from Lake Adger on the Green River to right here. We flipped the canoe in the first ten miles. I hurt my shoulder. Everything mildewed. We ran out of food." He looked over and smiled at his wife. She smiled back. She'd obviously heard the story many times before. "Best damn time of my life."

I pulled out the cell phone and had a rare four bars of service, so I called Chris.

"Hey, y'all," he answered. "Where the hell are you?"

"I'm looking up the boat ramp at my truck and your boat trailer."

"They're on the wrong damn river," I heard him say to Tom. "We've been looking for y'all all morning."

"We took a wrong turn. The river gods conspired against us."

"Paddle toward the sea," Chris said, still upbeat. "We'll find you before you get to the Intracoastal Waterway."

When we left the dock and U.S. 17 behind, the scenery began to change. We were deep in delta country, and vast expanses of marsh grass began to replace the forest. We hugged the channel bank. I heard the click and murmur of fiddler crabs ebbing and flowing over the mud flats. We still had the tide with us, but in less than an hour it would turn. We'd have to fight the flood of water washing upstream. I didn't want to think about how bad that would be. Decades earlier I'd been caught in Everglades National Park's Florida Bay in a canoe paddling against the tide. It had taken my paddling partner and me an hour to get out to our destination in the bay and three to get back. I didn't want to suffer the same fate again.

Steve and I began to stroke with more intensity. "Stroke, stroke," I repeated to myself as I paddled. "Stroke, stroke, stroke."

I looked back over my shoulder. Steve had his head down and each powerful stroke was stronger than anything I'd seen from him before. We had passed the spot where he had abandoned his paddle to the sea. Steve was like a horse who smelled the barn.

In 1981 he had made it as far as the U.S. 17 bridge then hid his canoe in the weeds and hitchhiked to McClellanville, a few miles south. A trucker picked him up and took him to a friend's house. After so many days on the river, Steve found the fishing village of McClellanville had seemed like a big city. Physically and emotionally exhausted, he showered, washed his hair and his clothes. "I plunged into a few situations that I would never ask another person to go into," he wrote in the final paragraph of his journal. "I'll have to save the unknowns for solo trips, which will hopefully only be for a few days, from now on."

I don't think Steve ever imagined he might be on this river so close to the sea again. I could feel in his direct and steady stroke pattern that he planned to make it this time.

We paddled hard for an hour until we heard a boat in the distance. As the filmmakers approached we could see Tom sitting at the stern at the throttle. With his sunglasses and brimmed cap he looked like an old salt who'd been running crab traps in the delta for years. Chris was standing up in the boat with the camera out, capturing the great "paddle to the sea" meeting in the Santee Delta. At two in the afternoon on day eleven we entered movie time.

"It's about thirty minutes until we the reach the Intracoastal Waterway," Chris yelled. "That's where we cross over from the North to the South Santee."

They motored ahead of us and shot footage of the canoe gliding along. The marsh formed a nice backdrop. We could tell we were approaching where the North Santee intersected the Intracoastal

Waterway when we saw the mast of a sailboat. It was under motor to our north, riding above the top of the marsh grass. Finally we could see the whole boat as it crossed the river, and then it disappeared back behind marsh grass to our south. The filmmakers' motorboat took a hard right turn and followed the sailboat up the waterway. The mast of the sailboat went a little farther along and then appeared in open water again for a brief second. "That's a short cut," Steve said, pointing to the tidal creek opening up to our right. "Let's cut this corner. God knows we need a break."

When we finally made the turn south into the Intracoastal Waterway I was struck by how straight and wide the route appeared. It was human engineering on a grand scale. The Intracoastal Waterway, a three-thousand-mile sheltered waterway down the East Coast from New Jersey to Brownsville, Texas, consists of a dredged route of natural inlets, bays, saltwater rivers, and sounds with man-made canals to connect them. We would paddle only a quarter-mile section of the waterway, but I knew that if the tide turned on us, this stretch could be our Waterloo.

Almost immediately our boat came to a dead stop as we hit the incoming tide. It was my nightmare scenario. We stroked for ten minutes and made no progress. Chris and Tom were almost out of sight ahead of us on the arrow-straight waterway. With each stroke I was more and more aware of my physical body, the only thing I had to transport me to the ocean. The lower quarter of my back had ached the whole trip, but after eleven days sitting upright in the canoe, I felt my muscles in knots and close to shutting down. My left shoulder throbbed, an old kayaking injury asserting itself after tens of thousands of repetitive paddle strokes. I knew at that moment why the old-time St. Lawrence River voyagers lived such short lives. They simply wore out.

I looked down at my feet, tanned except where the straps of my sandals crossed. My feet hurt from the wounds I'd suffered days earlier on the portage at Neal Shoals. The Band-Aids I'd put on my heels every night were gone, and the skin on all the blisters had turned white and puffy. All these physical infirmities were of little consequence, though, compared to the mental fatigue, which surged like the tide.

I looked back at Steve. He was feeling it too. I could see the doubt in his eyes, and he wasn't paddling as hard as he had been. Was this the end of our self-propelled journey?

Chris and Tom had turned around when they realized how far behind we had fallen, and soon the johnboat pulled alongside our motionless canoe. "Let's tow you up the waterway," Tom yelled. "Then we'll turn you loose again when we get to the South Santee and you can paddle the last few miles to the sea."

After all this, we were going to have to cheat to get the final three or four miles to the ocean. It didn't seem fair to come all this way under our own power and then near the end go by tow like a crippled schooner. I couldn't believe this was happening.

After uncoiling the rope from Venable's yellow throw bag, I tossed the knotted end to Chris. I rigged a double line from canoe to skiff, and Tom engaged the engine. As they hauled us slowly up the waterway, I sat sullen in the bow seat of the canoe. Chris was kind enough to keep the camera in the case, so there would be no record of our abject failure. I worried that when we got to the ocean they would insist that we fake our approach and act as if we had paddled all the way. I knew I couldn't do that, meaning Chris would have no ending for his film. At that moment our situation seemed more like the disappointments that adults are always telling kids to expect. "Real life" scuttles the best plans. Things fall apart. The center cannot hold, as Yeats said.

I looked back and Steve's wild blond hair was vertical in the artificial breeze. He had a smile on his face. "You have to admit it's pleasant being under power," he yelled into the wind.

Two miles later Tom turned us loose where the South Santee flooded into the Intracoastal Waterway. Once we unattached the rope and I'd stuffed it back in the sack, the skiff motored forward a hundred feet. I looked around. Upstream the quarter-mile-wide South Santee surged down from the upcountry to the sea. On the other side of the waterway, the river made a break for the ocean through acres of marsh.

Chris pulled out his camera and began to film. We ruddered downstream on the South Santee and quickly found we could make some progress against the tide. In a half-hour we had paddled a mile or so down the river. At this rate we would make it to the sea, still about two miles ahead. Neither of us spoke. There was a serious silence in the boat.

The skiff disappeared ahead. A half-hour later we approached the upstream point of Brown Island, a spit of marshy land separated from the river by a tidal stream. That meant we had a little more than a mile left to go. I could see that Chris and Tom were set up on the downstream point at the end of Brown Island to film us passing. Chris motioned for us to swing close to them. We were fifty feet off the point when two dolphins surfaced a few yards from the canoe, breaching between the camera and us. I felt like I could have reached out and touched them with the paddle. Chris stood straight up when they surfaced, more surprised than we were. "Money shot!" he yelled at the passing canoe. "I hope to hell that's in focus."

There was a big island named Grace right before the final turn to the sea. As we approached I had my last moment of doubt that we would make it. Behind us the filmmakers hurriedly loaded the gear into the skiff for the final sprint to Cedar Island Point, where they hoped to see us enter the ocean. Ahead of us I could see a long line of greening marsh and a gray corduroy sky. I was so tired. For a moment I didn't think we were moving at all. "We're stopped dead in the water again," I said, exasperated.

"No we're not," Steve said. "Look at a single point on the shore. Focus on it and you'll see we're making progress."

When we passed the low-lying, tide-swept point of Grace Island, we finally rounded the last turn on the South Santee. Steve and I both looked up from stroking, and there it was—the sea. Two bald eagles played above us, and we could see breakers in the distance. As if to create a bookend on our trip, a light rain began to fall.

We stroked forward into the cresting waves as hard as we could. A hundred more yards of open water. As we passed Tom and Chris on the point, they held up their arms as if we had just scored a touchdown, a signal that they were filming and to keep paddling. Then we knew it: We were in the open sea. I could hear the breakers up and down the coast. The skies were heavy and gray, the beach deserted. The laden canoe rode up and down on the rolling surf as we surveyed the South Carolina coast. To the south I could see the point of the Cape Romain National Wildlife Refuge. To the north were the outlines of Cedar Island, where the white-capped breakers of the incoming tide ate at the fragile land.

We pointed the canoe toward the beach at Santee Point and surfed it to shore. Neither of us had spoken a word since we had rounded the point. With our canoe on the sand, we stripped off life jackets, hats, sunglasses, and shirts and plunged into the cool, soothing salt water like two children who have seen the sea for the first time.

After playing in the water, I emerged and sat on the bow of the canoe and dried off in the wild sea wind. In a moment of ecstasy Steve sprinted up the Santee Point beach and returned with two conches. Still speechless, my friend held one to his chest and the other out to me, a memento of our paddle to the sea.

Journeys start with a single step, and river voyages with a single paddle stroke. Some have hardships and tragedy along the way, and others move along as smooth and steady as the lower Santee. Sometimes journeys do both, meandering back and forth between good and bad. All end at some destination. Sometimes—like Steve—you get a chance to return to a place that you visited long before. Other times you need simply to leave something behind and move on. Sometimes you finish where you hoped, as on our paddle to the sea. Sometimes the end takes you by surprise, like Jeremy in Costa Rica, and it's never clear until the last moment that your life will suddenly be settled unexpectedly, forever.

It had been only a little over three months since I'd left Costa Rica. Not a day had gone by that I had not replayed the chaotic and ultimately tragic scene that had unfolded on the Rio Reventazón. I had written e-mails to Jeremy's friends and paddling colleagues, and I'd tried from a great distance to track the story in the local papers through a translator friend. There wasn't much to track. After the initial report of the accident, which included a picture of Jeremy face down on the riverbank, the story disappeared. The translator told me that Costa Rica has a culture of forgetting and that the process was underway. But I could not forget. I had gone to paddle in Central America for a holiday family adventure, and what I got was a memory that troubled me like a bone-deep ache.

I sat on the bow plate of our canoe and looked up and down the beach. The sand below my bare feet had once been part of a mountain hundreds of miles to the west. Behind me, the ocean stretched thousands of miles farther than I could see. There was more than a little

Romantic in me, and I hoped that if the river remembered it would note that I was one of the few who had paddled its length.

Besides the friendship, it was the water I would remember. For millions of years the Santee had gathered the muddy flow of a thousand tributary streams and woven them into a single strand. In the broad delta the mighty river had broken into twin streams, and it was there we had lost our way. After recovering our bearings, we made the final few miles and found, at the Santee's mouth, that the river disappeared. But it wasn't gone. It had simply merged with the larger ocean.

Acknowledgments

Books, like rivers, have many origins. The headwaters of this narrative are two actual journeys, our December 2008 family paddling vacation in Costa Rica and my eleven-day trip down the Santee in March and April 2009. These trips offered the concrete outlines of the present narrative, but various texts also contributed to its texture and meaning.

In January 2006 I discovered a children's picture book published in 1941 called *Paddle-to-the-Sea* at the South Carolina Book Festival, and I began to imagine a trip from my backyard to the ocean. Written and illustrated by American author and artist Hölling C. Hölling, *Paddle-to-the-Sea* tells the story of a boy who carves a toy canoe with a wooden Indian paddling it. On the canoe's bottom the boy writes, "Please put me back in the water. I am Paddle-to-the-Sea," and drops it in Canada's Lake Nipigon. Paddle-to-the-Sea travels all the Great Lakes and finally reaches the Atlantic Ocean. Along the way the tiny, carved toy canoeist encounters and endures a sawmill, storms on the Great Lakes, a shipwreck, currents, a forest fire, a plunge over Niagara Falls, and large seagoing ships.

Paddle-to-the-Sea made an impact in the literary world and was recognized as a Caldecott Honor Book in 1942. Some argue it is an early ecology book because it introduced a whole generation of children to the idea of watersheds. Twenty years later, a film (also called

Paddle-to-the-Sea) was produced by the National Film Board of Canada and directed by Bill Mason of *Path of the Paddle* fame. It too had its success when it was nominated for an Oscar.

The tributaries feeding my narrative through the years of composition are various as its original sources. I consulted a variety of primary and secondary works for the factual and literary information: Robert Mills's *Atlas of the State* (1825); John Pendleton Kennedy's *Horse-Shoe Robinson* (1852); J. D. Bailey's *The History of Grindal Shoals* (1921); Arthur Henry Hirsch's *The Huguenots of Colonial South Carolina* (1928); Julia Peterkin's *Scarlet Sister Mary* (1928); W. J. Cash's *Mind of the South* (1941); Henry Savage's *River of the Carolinas: The Santee* (1956); William P. Cumming's *The Southeast in Early Maps* (1958; revised and enlarged by Louis De Vorsey Jr., 1998); Archibald Rutledge's *Deep River: Collected Poems* (1960); Bobby Gilmer Moss's *The Old Iron District* (1972); Walter Edgar's *History of Santee Cooper, 1934–1984* (1984) and *South Carolina: A History* (1998); Mike Hembree and Paul Crocker's *Glendale* (1994); Billy Kennedy's *The Scots-Irish in the Carolinas* (1997); David Taylor's "The Ned Beatty and Me" in *Upcountry Review* (Fall 1999); Rick Bass's "The Call of the Congaree" in *Sierra Magazine* (July/August 2002); Robert F. Durden's *Electrifying the Piedmont* (2003); Susan Millar Williams's biography of Julia Peterkin, *A Devil and a Good Woman Too* (2008); Vennie Deas-Moore's *Columbia's Riverbanks: A History of Its Waterways* (2008); and Robert Kapsch's *Historic Canals and Waterways of South Carolina* (2010).

I also used various Internet sources, common and obscure, including online applications for the National Register of Historic Places for the sites in the piedmont such as Pinckneyville, the Broad River's Fish Dam Ford, and the Lockhart Canal; I found "The Narrative of Richard Jones, a Boatman on the Broad River" in an interview conducted in Union County, South Carolina, by the Federal Writers' Project on July 9, 1937; the *New York Times* provided numerous articles about the Santee basin and particularly the rise of nuclear power in South Carolina in the 1960s and 1970s; and as noted in the narrative, the *South Carolina Gazetteer* was the source for my primary travel maps.

Above all, I'd like to thank Venable Vermont for paddling with me on the first leg of trip and for his river knowledge, friendship, support, Dutch-oven meals, spirit, colon blow, and world-class stories of rivers and river running; Steve Patton for his river journal, his friendship, his J-stroke, and for accompanying me on the final leg of a good river trip; Chris Cogan and Tom Byars for allowing the tables to be turned as in this narrative they become characters in my movie; Bernie Dunlap for predeparture stories about his uncle Henry Savage and keeping the Good Ship Wofford College on stable course; Wofford's academic dean David Wood for his support; Ron Robinson for the blessing; Cathy Conner for her wizardry with copying machines; George Fields for a lift down the hill to Grindal Shoals and good Daniel Morgan stories; Christine Swager for Revolutionary War context and for reading the Grindal Shoals section of the manuscript; Montana Stambaugh and the late Louie Philips for providing a dry porch for the river voyagers the first night on the river; Gray Cecil for logistical support; Zuble, Margie, and their girls for putting us up (and putting up with us) on our Columbia layover; Drake Perrow for the Santee shuttle; Tom's parents, the Byarses, for feeding us and putting us up at Murrell's Inlet on the night after we finally crawled off the river; Steve Jordan at Liquid Logic for a good deal on a sit-on-top kayak, even though I didn't end up using it; John Vermont for reading and river advice; Frank, Ken, Dunk, and Grady for our tune-up trip; Steve Liebig and Tom Visnius for reading the manuscript in the late stages and making important suggestions; Luís Fernando Allen at the Hotel Interamericano in Turrialba, Costa Rica, for helping us recover after our tragic river trip; Stuart Stevens for listening to my Costa Rica story; Laura Barbas-Rhoden for translating articles about Jeremy's death; Fred Parrish, as always, for his vast knowledge of all things natural in the watershed; Bob Cumming for sending me a copy of his father's book *The Southeast in Early Maps* and taking me to the Davidson College map room to see the originals; Wofford College archivist Philip Stone for first pointing me toward Duane A. Stober's 1969 "River Voyageurs" journal; Alan Stokes at the Caroliniana Library at the University of South Carolina for helping me sort through the Henry Savage records and letters; Susan Toms in Spartanburg County Library's Kennedy Room for sending me the March 31, 1880, piece in the *Carolina Spartan* about the Garner Brothers paddling from Skull Shoals to the sea; to UGA Press's Laura Sutton, Jon Davies, and all for the support they have shown me; and, finally, many thanks to my wife, Betsy, as always, for everything.